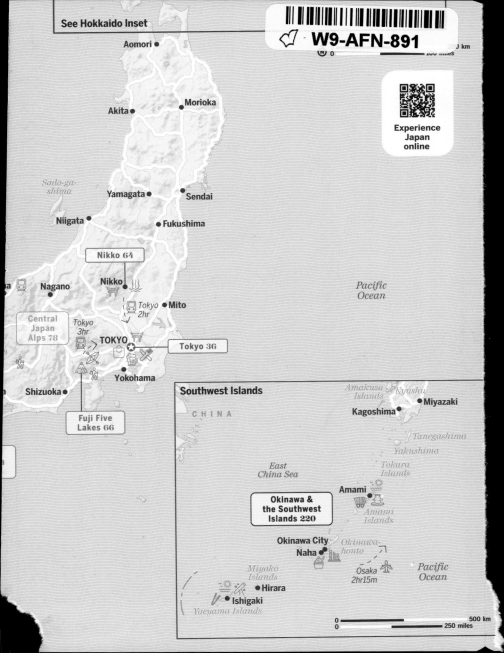

W9-AFN-891

Experience
Japan
online

Aomori

Morioka

Akita

Sado-ga-shima

Yamagata

Sendai

Niigata

Fukushima

Nikko 64

Nikko

Tokyo 2hr • Mito

Central Japan Alps 78

Tokyo 3hr

TOKYO

Tokyo 36

Nagano

Yokohama

Shizuoka

Fuji Five Lakes 66

Pacific Ocean

Southwest Islands

Amakusa Islands *Kyushu*

CHINA

Kagoshima • Miyazaki

Tanegashima

Yakushima

East China Sea

Tokara Islands

Amami

Okinawa & the Southwest Islands 220

Amami Islands

Okinawa City

Naha

Okinawa-honto

Miyako Islands

Osaka 2hr15m

Pacific Ocean

• Hirara

• Ishigaki

Yaeyama Islands

0   500 km
0   250 miles

▬▬▬ Meditate at serene temple gardens and make a pilgrimage through the mountains. Taste the finest sake and go on a journey of culinary delights. Walk the roads of samurai and shoguns to stand in the shadow of magnificent castles. Let the hot springs wash your worries away. Cruise down winter slopes and dive into glistening seas. Discover the ancient art of tea and meet your favourite pop-culture icons. See the sunrise at the peak of the mountain you just conquered.

This is Japan.

**TURN THE PAGE AND START PLANNING
YOUR NEXT BEST TRIP →**

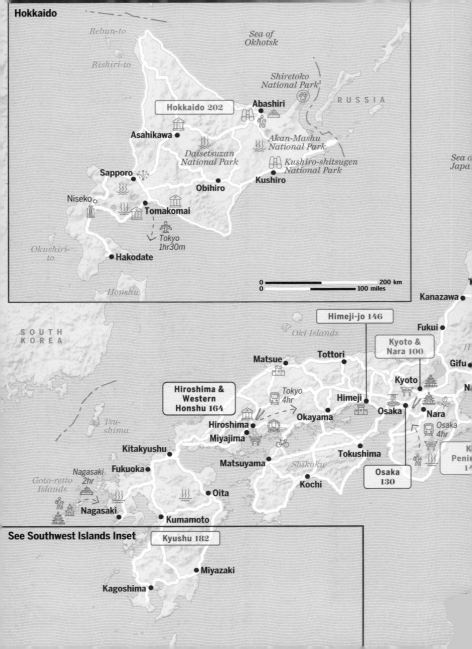

Lonely planet

JAPAN

Lucy Dayman, Tom Fay, Todd Fong,
Rebecca Milner, Winnie Tan, Ted Taylor

Contents

DR_FLASH/SHUTTERSTOCK ©

Above Arashiyama bamboo forest (p120), Kyoto.

PREVIOUS SPREAD: F11PHOTO/SHUTTERSTOCK ©

There are more than 30,000 ramen shops in Japan, over 3000 of which are in Tokyo.

In 2018, more than 380,000kL of sake was brewed in Japan.

HEARTY RAMEN,
SMOOTH SAKE

It's no exaggeration to say that Japan takes food seriously. For centuries, everything from raising the best cattle to concocting the perfect ramen broth has been elevated into an art form. There's something delicious to eat no matter where you go and, with the best locally sourced ingredients available, you can taste the seas, the pastures and even the mountains of Japan right at the dinner table.

URAIWONS/SHUTTERSTOCK ©

→ SIDE-ALLEY DINING

Tokyoites love their *yokocho*. The bar- and restaurant-filled alleyways are where they unwind on a Friday night, with *yakitori* (skewers) and cold beer.

▶ Learn more about *yokocho* on p48

Left Serving sake from a flask.
Right Omoide-yokocho (p48), Tokyo.
Below Bowl of ramen.

BIIRU!

Drop into any *izakaya* (pub-eatery) and you'll hear locals say *'Biiru, kudasai!'* (Beer, please!). Some prefectures even have their own signature brew.

▶ Read about Okinawa's Orion beer on p226
▶ Find Osaka's prime craft-beer brewery on p141

RIGHT: EYEEM/ALAMY STOCK PHOTO ©

↑ SLURP & BURP

Forget all you know about table manners at a ramen joint: loud slurping isn't just allowed, but encouraged. Join the locals in a noodle-sucking symphony.

▶ Visit every foodie's mecca, Osaka – home of ramen, *tako-yaki* and conveyor-belt sushi. (p130)

▶ Discover the secrets of Okinawa's long-living residents: salty 'sea grapes', fresh seafood and cold Orion beer. (p225)

▶ Stuff your stomach with the soul food of Hiroshima, *okonomiyaki*, expertly prepared before you by *okonomiyaki* masters. (p176)

▶ Try traditional Japanese cooking at its finest in Kyoto, the nation's capital of *kaiseki*. (p110)

▶ Sample street food and some of Japan's finest sake in Takayama's old town. (p84)

Japan has over 80,000 shrines. There are slightly fewer temples: over 70,000 countrywide.

In Kyoto alone, the number of shrines and temples combined exceeds 2800.

JOURNEY TO
ENLIGHTENMENT

Discover the world of Japanese religion and spirituality: join the ranks of ancient pilgrims as you embark on a holy trek through the mountains, or take a crash course in Shinto and Buddhism as you visit shrines and temples across the country. Step through the *torii* (red entrance gate) into the world of the sacred, and journey one step further to finding inner peace.

COWARDLION/SHUTTERSTOCK ©

Left Fushimi Inari Taisha shrine (p118), Kyoto.
Right Kokuzo Bosatsu statue, Todai-ji (p122), Nara.
Below Wooden *ema* at Meiji-jingu (p42), Tokyo.

→ TEMPLE OR SHRINE?

If there's a *torii*, it's a shrine. On the other hand, Buddhist temples house statues of deities, while shrines do not.

ETHICAL FOOD

Buddhist monks eat a vegetarian cuisine called *shojin-ryori*. Some temples serve it to guests too.

RIGHT, PABKOV/SHUTTERSTOCK ©

↑ LUCKY TALISMANS

Write your wishes on an *ema* or buy an *omamori* for protection – you'll find good luck and blessings at Japan's many holy sites.

▶ Learn more about *ema* (p117) and *omamori* (p173)

▶ Take a guided tour covering the culture and history of Koyasan, a mountain monastery on the Kii Peninsula. (p156)

▶ Bask in the grandeur of Shimane Prefecture's Izumo Taisha, one of Japan's most important shrines. (p170)

▶ Visit Meiji-jingu shrine and its gardens, a green oasis in the bustling heart of Tokyo. (p42)

▶ See Kyoto's iconic 'Golden Pavilion' (Kinkaku-ji), or find respite at smaller, serene shrines like Shoden-ji. (p116)

▶ Pay respects to the bronze Daibutsu (Great Buddha) of Todai-ji in Nara. (p122)

EDO
ESCAPADES

Scattered across the country are relics of a bygone era of shoguns and samurai. Explore the grand castles and noble quarters, but journey deep into the mountains and you'll also find remnants of an old, simpler way of life in rural villages and along winding, historical roads.

▶ Admire Japan's grandest castle, Himeji-jo. (p146)

▶ Find a quiet escape at Shirakawa-go, in remote villages unchanged for centuries. (p92)

▶ Walk the Yamanobe-no-michi, visiting historical sites on the way. (p126)

▶ Stroll around the Edo-period samurai town of Kitsuki in a kimono. (p193)

▶ Sail to Kudaka-jima in Okinawa, the birthplace of the Ryukyu kingdom. (p233)

LEFT MTAIRA/SHUTTERSTOCK © BELOW PIXHOUND/SHUTTERSTOCK ©

← **AGE OF SHOGUNS**

Many of the old castles and villages seen today are remnants of the Edo period (1603–1868), built during the rule of the Tokugawa shogunate.

→ **HOKKAIDO'S INDIGENOUS PEOPLE**

Hokkaido is home to an indigenous group called the Ainu. Today, there are approximately 17,000 Ainu living in the prefecture.

▶ Learn more about the Ainu on p216

Above Iwakuni-jo (p179).
Left Man in traditional Ainu dress (p216).
Right Kurokawa onsen (p188), Kyushu.

There are nearly 3000 onsen resorts in Japan.

The prefecture with the most onsen resorts is Hokkaido, with around 250.

VOLCANIC
BATHS

━━━ Japan's favourite way to relax is having a soak in an onsen (hot spring), followed by a cold glass of coffee-flavoured milk. However, onsen is more than just relaxation. Many believe in the waters' healing and beautifying powers, so it's no wonder the locals take a dip every chance they get.

▶ Achieve ultimate relaxation by going onsen-hopping at Kurokawa Onsen. (p189)

▶ See Jigoku-dani, the steaming 'hell valley' of Hokkaido, then visit Noboribetsu Onsen for a soak. (p215)

▶ Find the remote Kuronagi Onsen, hidden in the forests around Toyama. (p97)

DRYADPHOTOS/SHUTTERSTOCK ©

More than 200,000 people climb Mt Fuji every year.

There are 50,000 animal species in Japan, but only 279 of them are native.

Japan has over 600 varieties of cherry tree.

JOURNEY INTO
THE WILD

Miles of untouched wilderness, clear blue seas, a snow-capped Mt Fuji framed by *sakura* (cherry blossoms), – those are just some of the wonders you'll see when you take a trip through the Japanese countryside. Whether you hike, sail, swim or climb, the views awaiting you at the end will be well worth the journey.

Left Hiking Daisetsuzan (p212), Hokkaido.
Right Climbing the Yoshida Trail, Mt Fuji (p71).
Below Hanami parties, Ueno-koen (p51), Tokyo.

→ FAITH & MT FUJI

Mt Fuji has long held significance in Japanese religions like Shinto and Shugendo. Pilgrims have been climbing Mt Fuji as early as the Heian period (794–1185).

▶ Learn more about climbing Mt Fuji on p70

HOLY JOURNEY

Followers of the Japanese religion Shugendo practice by making pilgrimages through mountains and forests on foot.

▶ Learn more about Shugendo on p154

↑ SAKURA, SAKURA

The blooming of cherry blossoms signifies new beginnings, and the pink petals are ushered in with outdoor picnics called *hanami*.

▶ Read more about *sakura* on p114

▶ Hike to the summits of the Japan Alps and see the reflective lakes of Kamikochi. (p88)

▶ Swim and snorkel in the crystal-clear waters of the Yaeyama Islands. (p228)

▶ Spot brown bears and whales while cruising along the coast of Shiretoko National Park. (p210)

▶ Hike the Nakahechi Trail and make your way across the Kii Peninsula. (p154)

▶ Greet the sunrise at the summit of Japan's highest peak, Mt Fuji. (p73)

ADVENTURE
INCOMING

The best way to experience Japan is to dive right in – climb mountains, try out a new sport, sing in front of complete strangers. Japan has plenty of surprises in store for the traveller who isn't afraid to stray from convention; all you need is a sense of adventure.

RUSSIA

Nakasendo Trail
Journeyman's road
The 9km forest trail that connects two Edo-period post towns is tranquil and beginner friendly. Reward yourself afterwards with some tea and Japanese sweets in Tsumago or Magome, depending on where you start.

🚃 2hr from Nagoya
▶ p86

NORTH KOREA

Sea of Japan

SOUTH KOREA

Oki-shoto

Kanazawa

Matsue

Kyoto
Nagoya

Okayama   Kobe
Hiroshima   Osaka

Tsu-shima

Takamatsu

Shimanami Kaido
Island-hopping on two wheels
Rent a bicycle and begin your journey through a cluster of islands, enjoying the salty sea breeze and expansive coastal views. Visit temples and parks along the way, and when you're hungry, drop by some of the local shops for a snack.

🚃 1hr from Hiroshima
▶ p174

Fukuoka   Matsuyama
                        Kochi
Goto-retto   Shikoku

Nagasaki   Kumamoto

Kyushu   Pacific
                         Ocean
Kagoshima   Miyazaki

TERENCE TOH CHIN ENG/SHUTTERSTOCK ©,
DOWRAIK/SHUTTERSTOCK ©,
OFFICE(ANIGAWA/SHUTTERSTOCK ©

See Southwest Islands Inset

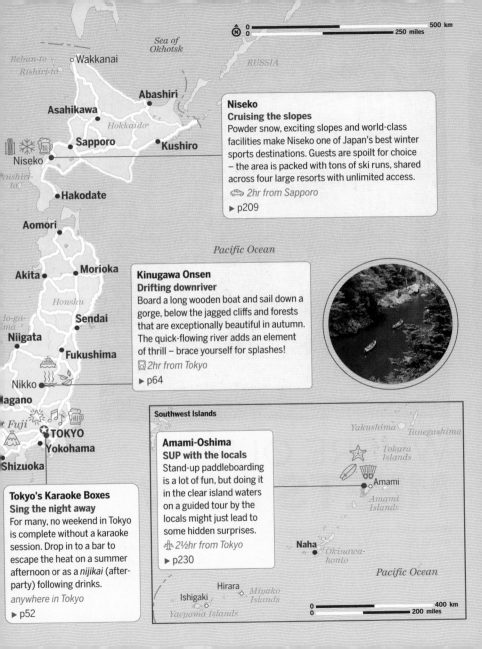

Sea of Okhotsk

RUSSIA

500 km
250 miles

Rebun-tō
Rishiri-tō

Wakkanai

Abashiri

Asahikawa

Hokkaidō

Sapporo

Kushiro

Niseko

Kushiri-tō

Hakodate

Niseko
Cruising the slopes
Powder snow, exciting slopes and world-class facilities make Niseko one of Japan's best winter sports destinations. Guests are spoilt for choice – the area is packed with tons of ski runs, shared across four large resorts with unlimited access.

🚗 *2hr from Sapporo*

▶ p209

Aomori

Pacific Ocean

Akita

Morioka

Honshu

Io-ga-ma

Sendai

Niigata

Fukushima

Kinugawa Onsen
Drifting downriver
Board a long wooden boat and sail down a gorge, below the jagged cliffs and forests that are exceptionally beautiful in autumn. The quick-flowing river adds an element of thrill – brace yourself for splashes!

🚃 *2hr from Tokyo*

▶ p64

Nikko

Nagano

Fuji

TOKYO

Yokohama

Shizuoka

Southwest Islands

Yakushima
Tanegashima

Tokara Islands

Amami-Oshima
SUP with the locals
Stand-up paddleboarding is a lot of fun, but doing it in the clear island waters on a guided tour by the locals might just lead to some hidden surprises.

✈ *2½hr from Tokyo*

▶ p230

Amami

Amami Islands

Naha

Okinawa-hontō

Pacific Ocean

Tokyo's Karaoke Boxes
Sing the night away
For many, no weekend in Tokyo is complete without a karaoke session. Drop in to a bar to escape the heat on a summer afternoon or as a *nijikai* (after-party) following drinks.

anywhere in Tokyo

▶ p52

Hirara
Miyako Islands

Ishigaki

Yaeyama Islands

400 km
200 miles

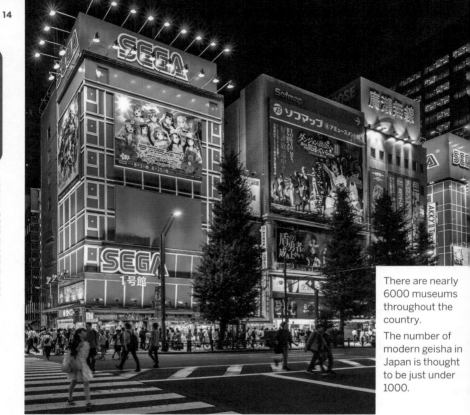

There are nearly 6000 museums throughout the country.

The number of modern geisha in Japan is thought to be just under 1000.

WHERE OLD
MEETS NEW

▰▰▰▰ Millions of people around the world consider themselves fans of Japanese culture, from the ancient art of tea to modern anime and manga. You won't have to travel too far to find it all – in a country where heritage both old and new blend seamlessly together, a culturally enriching experience is always right around the corner.

OSAZE CUOMO/SHUTTERSTOCK ©

→ ULTIMATE ENTERTAINERS

Aspiring geisha spend about six years learning their craft while being trained in music, dance, etiquette and tea ceremony.

▶ Learn more about geisha on p108

Left Akihabara (p45), Tokyo.
Right *Maiko* performance (p108), Kyoto.
Below *Yurukyara*, Hokkaido (p202).

TRADITIONAL SPOOKS

Yokai (fictional monsters) are alive in both traditional and pop culture of Japan. Spot them on everything from woodblock prints to anime.

▶ Read more about *yokai* on p90

RIGHT A JUSA113/SHUTTERSTOCK ©
KEY FRANCESCO BONINA/ALAMY STOCK PHOTO ©

▶ **Experience the quiet meditativeness and Zen spirit of a traditional tea ceremony in Kyoto.** (p106)

▶ **Immerse yourself in Japanese pop culture at the Ghibli Museum, Mitaka or Akihabara in Tokyo.** (p44)

▶ **See master swordsmith Matsunaga at his workshop in Arao, Kumamoto.** (p193)

▶ **Spend a night with the locals at a traditional *gassho-zukuri* house in Shirakawa-go.** (p92)

▶ **Take an immersive look at Hokkaido's native Ainu culture at Upopoy National Ainu Museum.** (p216)

↑ MASCOT OBSESSION

Japan has a mascot for just about everything – companies, stations, even prefectures. They're called *yurukyara*, a combination of the words *yuru* (soft, fluffy) and *kyara* (character).

Japanese schoolchildren are on summer break from mid-July to end of August. Marine Day (third Monday in July) creates a long weekend and Mountain Day on 11 August is also a public holiday.

↙ Island Escape

Okinawa is a summer hotspot. Try the Amami Islands for equally beautiful beaches with far less traffic.

● Amami-Oshima, p230

▸ amami-tourism.org

Demand for accommodation peaks during Obon week (mid-August). Book tours and overnight adventures in advance.

▸ lonelyplanet.com/japan/activities

Buy a folding fan or handheld motor fan to cool down during Japan's notoriously humid summers.

JUNE

Average daytime max: 27°C

JULY

Japan in
SUMMER

NITA LIMO/SHUTTERSTOCK ©, MI7/SHUTTERSTOCK ©, VARANDAH/SHUTTERSTOCK ©, SADAO/SHUTTERSTOCK ©, SHENYANG'S PHOTO. ALL RIGHTS RESERVED/GETTY IMAGES ©

↘ Walk on the Wild Side

Go hiking in Japan's largest national park in summer, when trails are largely snow-free.

📍 Daisetsuzan, p212
▶ daisetsuzan.or.jp

↑ Alpine Adventures

Escape the ruthless city heat and go camping and hiking at Kamikochi in the Japan Alps.

📍 Kamikochi, p88
▶ kamikochi.org

From early June to mid-July, spot hydrangeas blooming everywhere from large parks to residential areas.

AUGUST

Days of rainfall: 13

Average daytime max: 30°C
Days of rainfall: 12

← Lighting Up the Sky

Fireworks festivals are popular in summer. Locals go in *yukata*, a summer kimono-like attire.

🧳 Packing Notes

A hat, plenty of sunscreen, and a face towel to help keep the sweat off.

Check out a full calendar of events

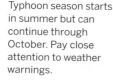

Typhoon season starts in summer but can continue through October. Pay close attention to weather warnings.

← All Aboard for Kurobe Gorge

Roll through the deep ravines on the Kurobe Gorge Railway and see the magnificent autumn foliage anytime from mid-October to November.

📍 Kurobe Kyokoku, p96
▶ kurotetu.co.jp

Demand for accommodation peaks during autum-foliage week, from late October through November. Book tours and overnight adventures in advance.

▶ lonelyplanet.com/japan/activities

Japan's quintessential autumn leaf is the *momiji* (Japanese maple), found in abundance around temples and parks.

SEPTEMBER

Average daytime max: 28°C

OCTOBER

Japan in
AUTUMN

POND THANANAT/SHUTTERSTOCK ©, OL_DMI/SHUTTERSTOCK ©,
KAI KEISUKE/SHUTTERSTOCK ©, KITTICHAI/SHUTTERSTOCK ©,
ALEX SEGRE/ALAMY STOCK PHOTO ©

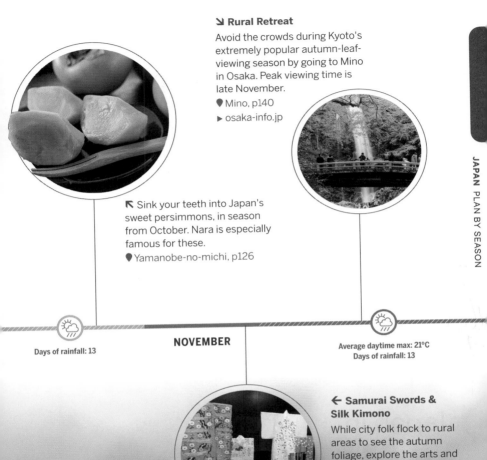

↘ Rural Retreat

Avoid the crowds during Kyoto's extremely popular autumn-leaf-viewing season by going to Mino in Osaka. Peak viewing time is late November.

📍 Mino, p140
▶ osaka-info.jp

↖ Sink your teeth into Japan's sweet persimmons, in season from October. Nara is especially famous for these.

📍 Yamanobe-no-michi, p126

NOVEMBER

Days of rainfall: 13

Average daytime max: 21°C
Days of rainfall: 13

← Samurai Swords & Silk Kimono

While city folk flock to rural areas to see the autumn foliage, explore the arts and culture of Tokyo at the Tokyo National Museum.

▶ Tokyo National Museum, p50
▶ tnm.jp

🧳 Packing Notes

Keep a jacket or your favourite clothing layers on hand for chillier nights.

The period after Christmas and the first week of January is the Japanese New Year holidays. Many shops and restaurants are closed nationwide.

↖ Sapporo Snow Festival

See giant snow sculptures and join in the fun at the Sapporo Snow Festival, over a week in early February.

📍 Sapporo, p209

▶ snowfes.com

Demand for accommodation peaks during Christmas and the Lunar New Year (late January to early February). Book tours and overnight adventures in advance.

▶ lonelyplanet.com/japan/activities

Japanese strawberries are the sweetest in January but are available from December through to May.

DECEMBER

Average daytime max: 12°C

JANUARY

Japan in
WINTER

STOCK_SHOT/SHUTTERSTOCK ©, VAPADI/SHUTTERSTOCK ©,
CAGE/SHUTTERSTOCK ©, MIXA/GETTY IMAGES ©, WENILIOU/SHUTTERSTOCK ©

↘ Snowy Villages

The winter light-up event at Ogimachi village in Shirakawa-go is a storybook cottage scene come to life. Expect crowds.

● Ogimachi, p95
▶ ml.shirakawa-go.org/en

↓ Eat Your Way Through the Islands

Instead of a holiday in the snow, go the other route and take a food trip through subtropical Okinawa.

● Okinawa-honto, p224
▶ visitokinawa.jp

For those long days out in the cold, disposable pocket warmers called *kairo* (カイロ) are cheaply available at convenience stores.

JAPAN PLAN BY SEASON

❄
Days of rainfall: 9

FEBRUARY

🌧
Average daytime max: 11°C
Days of rainfall: 7

← Relax in an Onsen

One of the best winter experiences is having a bath out in the snow in a *rotemburo* (outdoor bath). Available at most ryokan.

🧳 Packing Notes

Thermal underclothes and a down jacket; sturdy boots or ice cleats for rural areas with heavy snow.

Golden Week is packed with public holidays, from late April to the beginning of May. Large crowds everywhere.

↙ Nombe Sake Festival

Takayama's Nombe Sake Festival takes place in March, when local breweries unveil their first brews of the season.

● Takayama, p84

▶ hida-nombe.jp

Demand for accommodation peaks during cherry-blossom season (late March to early April). Book tours and overnight adventures in advance.

▶ lonelyplanet.com/japan/activities

See the magenta plum blossom from late February to early March, with cherry blossoms soon after.

MARCH

Average daytime max: 16°C

APRIL

Japan in
SPRING

TUGH/SHUTTERSTOCK ©, JENS_PAYLESS/SHUTTERSTOCK ©, TAKASHI IMAGES/SHUTTERSTOCK ©, TUKTA SIMO43/SHUTTERSTOCK ©, BLACKRABBIT3/SHUTTERSTOCK ©

↘ Pedalling the Petals

Cycle around Kyoto to chase down the cherry blossoms, riding along old paths and rivers as you go.

📍 Kyoto, p112

▶ kctp.net

↖ Hanami Heaven

During *sakura* season, many convenience stores sell tarp sheets for impromptu cherry-blossom-viewing parties.

📍 Ueno-koen, p51

▶ www.ueno-bunka.jp

MAY

Days of rainfall: 14

Average daytime max: 18°C
Days of rainfall: 13

↙ Peonies at Yushien

Marvel at a sea of vibrant blooming peonies at Yushien, a Japanese-style garden on an island in the middle of Lake Nakaumi.

📍 Yushien, p181

▶ yuushien.com

🧳 Packing Notes

A thick jacket for cold nights, and a small umbrella for spring showers.

KANTO
Trip Builder

TAKE YOUR PICK OF MUST-SEES AND HIDDEN GEMS

The Kanto region is the perfect sampler of everything Japan has to offer – vibrant city life, culture and gorgeous nature. Tokyo itself provides endless experiences, but ultra-convenient public transport means taking short trips out of the city is easy-peasy.

🗺 Trip Notes

Hub town Tokyo

How long Allow 10 days

Getting around Train and subway will get you anywhere within Tokyo and to neighbouring prefectures. For more flexibility on the outskirts, rent a car.

Tips Avoid taking the train in Tokyo during the morning rush hour between 7.30am and 9am. Highways in and out of the city can get congested in the evening from 5pm to 7.30pm.

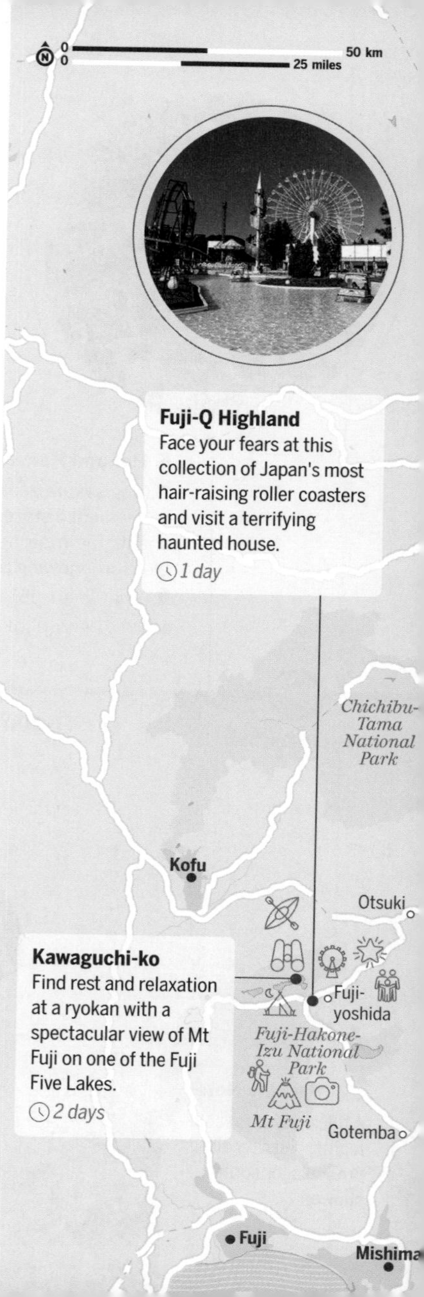

BLANSCAPE/SHUTTERSTOCK ©, J. HENNING BUCHHOLZ/SHUTTERSTOCK ©,

Fuji-Q Highland
Face your fears at this collection of Japan's most hair-raising roller coasters and visit a terrifying haunted house.
🕐 *1 day*

Chichibu-Tama National Park

Kofu

Otsuki

Kawaguchi-ko
Find rest and relaxation at a ryokan with a spectacular view of Mt Fuji on one of the Fuji Five Lakes.
🕐 *2 days*

○ Fuji-yoshida

Fuji-Hakone-Izu National Park

Mt Fuji   Gotemba ○

● Fuji   Mishima

0 — 50 km
0 — 25 miles

Nikko
See beautiful autumn foliage and the extravagant shrine of Tosho-gu, a World Heritage Site just two hours by train from the city.
🕐 *2 days*

Ueno
Spend an afternoon immersed in art and history at some of Tokyo's largest museums, including the Tokyo National Museum.
🕐 *1 day*

Mitaka
Take a breather in this quieter part of town, home to the Ghibli Museum, Mitaka and Inokashira-koen, one of Tokyo's best parks.
🕐 *½ day*

Ryogoku
Book tickets to see sumo wrestling at Japan's largest sumo stadium, or learn about the city's history at the Edo-Tokyo Museum.
🕐 *½ day*

Odaiba
Browse malls and other fun attractions on an artificial island in Tokyo Bay – a place to unleash your inner child.
🕐 *1 day*

Shibuya
Experience peak city life in Tokyo – there are plenty of places to eat and shop, and *yokocho* (alleyways) to explore.
🕐 *½ day*

Nikko National Park
Nikko
Imaichi
Utsunomiya
Mashiko
Maebashi
Mito
akasaki
Oyama
Shimodate
Kumagaya
Kasukabe
Kashiwa
hichibu
Ome
TOKYO ★
Hachioji
Chiba
Sagamihara
Kawasaki
Tokyo Bay
Ichihara
Kisarazu
Odawara
Boso Peninsula
Katsuura

CHUBU
Trip Builder

TAKE YOUR PICK OF MUST-SEES AND HIDDEN GEMS

Japan's middle region, Chubu, is defined by mountain ridges, untouched forests and remote villages. It's the ultimate destination for outdoor lovers, or someone looking to escape the metropolis for a while. Pack your hiking boots.

🗺 Trip Notes

Hub town Nagoya

How long Allow 10 to 12 days

Getting around Travel between prefectures by limited-express trains or shinkansen (bullet train). For rural destinations, take buses. Families can consider renting a car for easier travel.

Tips This region experiences heavy snow and strong winds. Be extra cautious if you're driving, and ask for a rental car with snow tyres.

NISHIHAMA/SHUTTERSTOCK ©, TUMSUBIN/SHUTTERSTOCK ©,
JANANYA SRIPHAIROT/SHUTTERSTOCK ©

0 — 50 km
0 — 25 miles

Toya
war

Takaoka   Toya

Kanazawa

Shirakawa-go
Wake up surrounded by mountain in the quiet villages of Shirakawa-go, and experience the slow, serene pace of life for a while.
🕐 *3–4 days*

Ogimachi   *Shirakawa-go*   Hida

Haku San National Park

Takayam

Nagoya
Feast on lots of tasty food options here in Chubu's largest city. A favourite local speciality is *tebasaki* (chicken wings).
🕐 *½ day*

Gifu

Ogaki

Ichinomiya

Tajimi

Kasugai

Seto

Nagoya

Kuwana

Toyota

Toyama

See the splendours of nature as you drive past imposing walls of snow or take a rail trip across a beautiful rocky gorge.

🕐 *2 days*

Karuizawa

Nagano

Go camping or hiking in Kamikochi, a favourite among locals for outdoor activities, or have a relaxing holiday in the resort town of Karuizawa.

🕐 *3–4 days*

Yamanashi Trails

Try the numerous hiking trails around Mt Fuji, or even climb Japan's revered mountain and highest peak itself in summer.

🕐 *2–3 days*

ozu

Tateyama

Hakuba

Nagano

Shinano-omachi

Chubu-Sangaku National Park

Kamikochi

Azumino

Matsumoto

Shiojiri

Suwa

Narai

Aidara

Chichibu-Tama National Park

Iida

Minami Alps National Park

Fuji-yoshida

Fuji-Hakone-Izu National Park

Mt Fuji

Gotemba

Fuji

Numazu

Shizuoka

KANSAI
Trip Builder

TAKE YOUR PICK OF MUST-SEES AND HIDDEN GEMS

A visit to Kansai, the centre of old Japanese traditions and culture, will most certainly be an enriching one. Not only will you deepen your understanding of Japanese history, you get to treat yourself to some of the nation's best dishes too.

Trip Notes

Hub towns Osaka, Kyoto

How long Allow 9 to 12 days

Getting around Most spots in this region are accessible by train or shinkansen from Osaka. Cycling is a great way to see Kyoto. Use either the public bus or a rental car around the Kii Peninsula.

Tips Discover some real gems by walking around the cities of Osaka and Kyoto, but be warned that they are among the hottest places in Japan in summer.

MIRKO KUZMANOVIC/SHUTTERSTOCK ©,
PATRICK FOTO/SHUTTERSTOCK ©, SUPERJOSEPH/SHUTTERSTOCK ©

○ Toyook
● Tottori

Himeji
Explore the grounds and buildings of Himeji-jo, the grandest of only 12 preserved original castles from Japan's feudal era.
① 1 day

○ Sayo

Nishiwa

○ Kasai

Himeji ●

○ Ako

● Kakoga

Osaka
Chow down on soul food and slurp some hearty ramen under the neon lights of Dotombori – especially vibrant at night.
① 1 day

Akashi

Sum
○

JAPAN BUILD YOUR TRIP

Mino
Enjoy nature and craft beer just outside Osaka – take woodland walks and reward yourself with a pint of Minoh beer afterwards.
🕐 1 day

Kyoto
Experience Japan's old traditions of geisha, tea ceremony, shrines and temples and more in its first capital city.
🕐 3 days

Nara
Make friends with the wild deer that roam freely around Nara-koen, a verdant park in this historical city.
🕐 1 day

Kii Peninsula
Go on a spiritual journey through forests and mountains following the ancient Kumano Kodo network of roads.
🕐 2–4 days

Miyazu

Nagoya
Kuwana
Yokkaichi

Kyoto   Otsu   Kusatsu

Sanda
Kawanishi   Mino

Uji

Kobe   Osaka

Nara

Haibara

Osaka-wan   Sakai

Kishiwada

Sennan   Hashimoto   Gojo

Iwade

Wakayama   Koya-san

Kii-nagashima

Arida

Owase

Gobo

Kumano

Hongu

Takijiri-oji

Shingu

Tanabe

Nachi-Katsuura
Kii-Katsuura

Kushimoto

Ⓝ 0 ___ 50 km
    0 ___ 25 miles

KYUSHU & THE SOUTHERN ISLANDS
Trip Builder

**TAKE YOUR PICK OF MUST-SEES
AND HIDDEN GEMS**

▬▬▬ The southern region of Japan can be overlooked by travellers, but it's where you'll have experiences unlike anywhere else in the country. Visit some of the most significant cities in modern Japanese history, or sink your toes into white beaches of pristine islands.

🗺 Trip Notes

Hub towns Fukuoka, Hiroshima

How long Allow 12 to 14 days

Getting around Trains, buses and cars are all options around Kyushu. Take short flights to the islands, then get around by car.

Tips Heavy traffic jams and difficulty finding parking are common issues in Okinawa. Leave early, and stay clear of the bus-only lanes on the left side.

PHOTO_J/SHUTTERSTOCK ©, LUCIANO MORTULA/SHUTTERSTOCK ©,
KHUN TA/SHUTTERSTOCK ©

⊕Ⓝ 0 ——— 200 km
0 ——— 100 miles

Goto-retto
Go hiking and cycling around these scenic islands and take in the coastal views, or try stand-up paddleboarding.
🕐 *1 day*

Korea Strait   *Tsushima*
   ○ Tsushima

Shimonos
Iki   **Kitakyushu** ●
Iki ○   **Fukuoka**   Bu
Hirado ●   ●**Karatsu**   H
   Kashima   **Kurum**
Goto-retto Islands   **Sasebo** ●   **Omuta**
   Nagasaki   **Kumam**
○ Fukue   Shimabara   **Yatsus**
Amakusa Islands   Hondo
   Shim   Hitoy
   ○ Izumi
Nagasaki   **Miyakonc**
Hop on a tram and   *Koshiki*   **Kirishima**
explore the rich culture   *Islands*   ●
of this coastal city, once a   **Kagoshima** ●   **Kar**
prominent port of foreign   Makurazaki ○
trade from the 1600s.   ○ Ibusu
🕐 *2–3 days*

   Osumi Stra
   Nishinoom
   Tanegashima
   Miyanoura
   Yakushima ○ Amb
   Osu
   Islan

   Tokara Islands

**See Southern
Islands Inset**

Shimane
Experience Japanese religion and history at Izumo Taisha and Matsue-jo in this sparsely populated coastal prefecture with charm.
⏱ 2 days

Hiroshima
Visit a city steeped in history and culture, with historic landmarks like Miyajima's floating *torii* (gate) and the Atomic Bomb Dome.
⏱ 2–3 days

Oita
Spend an entire day bath-hopping to your heart's content in one of Japan's most renowned onsen towns, Beppu.
⏱ 1–2 days

Pacific Ocean

Southern Islands

Yaeyama Islands
Go on an ultimate tropical-island getaway to the land of sandy beaches, green forests and starry night skies.
⏱ 1–2 days

Amami-Oshima
Have a go at traditional folk crafts like mud-dyeing and swim with giant sea turtles on this laid-back island.
⏱ 1–2 days

Okinawa-honto
Sample the local cuisine while you explore the island and its beaches – its warm climate makes it Japan's favourite winter destination.
⏱ 2–3 days

0 ——— 200 km
0 ——— 100 miles

Okinoshima Dogo
Nishino-shima *Oki Islands*
Matsue
Oda Izumo
Niimi
Hamada
Miyoshi Ako Himeji Kyoto
Masuda Okayama Kobe Osaka Nara
Fukuyama Kurashiki Akashi Nara
Onomichi *Awaji-shima*
aguchi Hiroshima Takamatsu Sumoto
Kure Wakayama
Hofu Iwakuni *Kii Peninsula*
Kudamatsu
sa Yawatahama Tanabe
pu Kitsuki Uwajima
Oita
Taketa Saiki
Takachiho
eoka
yuga
yazaki
shima

Amami-Oshima
Amami Islands Naze
Kikai-jima
Tokunoshima
Okinoerabu-jima
Kume-jima Nago
Naha *Okinawa Islands*
Kerama Islands

Miyako Islands
Ishigaki-jima
Miyako-jima
Ishigaki
Yaeyama Islands

7 Things to Know About
JAPAN

INSIDER TIPS TO HIT THE GROUND RUNNING

1 Crazy Commute

For Tokyoites, the morning commute is a contact sport. On weekdays from 7.30am to 9am, millions squeeze into trains across the city, sometimes helped along by station staff who make sure everyone's packed in. Shinjuku Station, the busiest in the world, sees an average of over 3.5 million commuters a day; there are more than 200 exits leading in and out of the complex.

▶ See more about travelling around Tokyo on p40

2 Public Etiquette

Avoid speaking loudly on public transport. Always ride on one side of the escalator – left in Kanto, right in Kansai. Rubbish bins are few and far between, so take your trash back with you. All food waste, wrappings and paper go with burnable trash, while clean plastic is non-burnable trash.

▶ See more about travel essentials on p248

3 Edible Souvenirs

They are called *omiyage* – food meant for gifting. Locals buy them for family, friends or co-workers, but you can enjoy them yourself!

▶ See classic *omiyage* on p225

4 The Proper Way to Pay

Don't hand money to the cashier – always place your cash or credit card on the tray in front of you.

▶ See more about managing money on p243

ROB ZS/SHUTTERSTOCK ©, VOVA_31/SHUTTERSTOCK ©; SOFIJA DJUKIC/SHUTTERSTOCK ©,
SERGIO YONED/SHUTTERSTOCK ©, NAZARII M/SHUTTERSTOCK ©, DEAWSS/SHUTTERSTOCK ©,
DJENT/SHUTTERSTOCK ©, YUKIMCO/SHUTTERSTOCK ©.

5 Getting Around After Hours

There's no 24-hour public transport in Japan. The trains in Tokyo run until 1am at the latest, and you'll want to be at the station well before the last train. If you miss it, the alternative is to catch a taxi, but they can be expensive.

▶ See more about getting around on p240

6 Local Lingo

Here are some Japanese words that will come in handy when dining out:

omori – large portion (often free at ramen stalls)

namimori – regular portion

okawari – refill

mochikaeri – takeaway

tennai de – eat-in

Foreigners usually get a free pass, but politeness is imperative in Japanese culture and language. Here's how to be respectful to a local:

onegai shimasu – Follow up any of your orders or requests with this. For example, if you want tea, say *'Ocha onegai shimasu'*.

arigato gozaimasu – Because it's a bit of a mouthful, some may be tempted to shorten it to simply *arigato*. This is fine when said among friends, but take the time to thank a helpful local the right way.

▶ See the Language chapter on p250

7 Braving the Elements

Japan experiences gruelling summers and chilly winters. You'll be doing a lot of walking too, especially if you're in the city. Be sure to carry these items with you:

Folding umbrella with UV blocking For sudden showers and sweltering heat.

Cooling wipes Buy these at the pharmacy to wipe away the sweat and stick.

Pocket warmer Effectively warms cold hands; adhesive ones stick to the inside of your coat.

▶ See more about the seasons on p16

Read, Listen, Watch & Follow

📖 **READ**

Convenience Store Woman (Sayaka Murata; 2016)
A woman figures out how she fits into society's standards.

Grotesque (Natsuo Kirino; 2003) A look at the outcasts and the dark underside of Japanese society.

No Longer Human (Osamu Dazai; 1948) A man struggles to come to terms with his humanity.

Rashomon and Seventeen Other Stories (Ryunosuke Akutagawa; 2009) Tales by Japan's most prominent short-story writer.

🎧 **LISTEN**

Pop Virus (Hoshino Gen; 2018) Funky tunes to dance to, with cheerful, catchy hooks that stay in your head.

Cycle Hit 1991– 1997 Complete Single Collection (Spitz; 2006) Iconic songs from the pop band's long career that you'll hear at every karaoke bar in Tokyo.

Your Name (Radwimps; 2016) Everything from energetic anthems to moving ballads by one of Japan's most popular bands (pictured right).

Singles 2000 (Miyuki Nakajima; 2002) A compilation of timeless melodies from Japan's most recognisable singer-songwriter.

(IMAGINECHINA LIMITED/ALAMY STOCK PHOTO ©

Abroad in Japan (abroadinjapan.com) Podcast discussing culture, current events and all things weird and wacky happening in Japan.

▷ WATCH

Shoplifters (2018) A family with a penchant for shoplifting navigates a life of poverty on Tokyo's outskirts.

The Wind Rises (2013) Based on the story of Jiro Horikoshi, who designed some of Japan's WWII fighter aircraft.

Departures (2008) An aspiring musician turned ritual undertaker finds new life in his work.

Jiro Dreams of Sushi (2011) Sushi artistry at Ginza's restaurant Sukiyabashi Jiro with sushi master, Jiro Ono.

Rashomon (1950) Akira Kurosawa's movie adaptation of the famous tale of unreliable narrators.

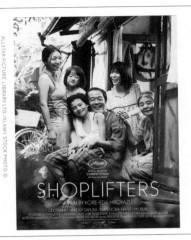

ALLSTAR PICTURE LIBRARY LTD./ALAMY STOCK PHOTO ©

◯ FOLLOW

Tokyo Weekender
(tokyoweekender.com)
Japan's oldest English-language magazine.

METROPOLIS
Metropolis Japan
(metropolisjapan.com)
Culture, events, travel and more.

Storied
(storiedmag.com)
Stunning images and amazing stories from all over Japan.

Tokyo Gig Guide
(tokyogigguide.com)
Comprehensive list of live music events.

@visitjapanjp
Official account of Japan National Tourism Organisation.

Sate your Japan dreaming with a virtual vacation at lonelyplanet.com/japan# planning-a-trip

TOKYO

CITY LIFE | CULTURE | ART

Experience
Tokyo
online

Bonus Online Experiences

▶ **Connecting Through Karaoke**

▶ **The Otaku's Guide to Tokyo**

Visit the enchanting
Ghibli Museum, Mitaka
(p45)
🕐 ½ day

Inokashira-koen

Enjoy a laid-back weekend picnic in Tokyo's favourite park, **Yoyogi-koen** (p60)
🕐 ½ day

New York Bar

TOKYO
Trip Builder

▬▬▬ Tokyo, the capital of Japan, is the country's largest city and also one of the world's largest. Everything you could possibly want in terms of the urban Japan experience, you can have it here, and have it in spades: superlative restaurants, statement architecture, trend-setting boutiques, hole-in-the-wall bars, giant LED displays and flashing neon lights. More than any one sight, it's the city itself – a sprawling, organic thing, stretching as far as the eye can see – that enchants visitors.

Explore bookable experiences in Tokyo online

Walk the narrow lanes of the historic, artsy **Yanaka** neighbourhood (p58)
🕐 ½ day

See masterpieces of Japanese art and artisanship at the **Tokyo National Museum** (p50)
🕐 ½ day

Ueno-koen

Experience Tokyo's traditional side at Shinto shrine **Meiji-jingu** (p42)
🕐 *2 hours*

Shinjuku-gyoen

Fukiage Imperial Gardens

Meiji-jingu-gyoen

Akasaka Imperial Property

Shop (or window-shop) your way through fashionable **Ginza** (p54)
🕐 *½–1 day*

Explore Shibuya, starting with its famous intersection, **Shibuya Crossing** (p47)
🕐 *½ day*

Toyosu Market

Go for a meal in one of Tokyo's atmospheric dining alleyways, like **Ebisu-yokocho** (p49)
🕐 *2 hours*

Tokyo Bay

N
0   4 km
0   2 miles

YANNICK LUTHY/ALAMY STOCK PHOTO ©
PICTURE CELLS/SHUTTERSTOCK ©
NOR GAL/SHUTTERSTOCK ©, KORKUSUNG/
SHUTTERSTOCK ©, SEAN PAVONE/SHUTTERSTOCK ©

Practicalities

WINDS/SHUTTERSTOCK ©

ARRIVING

Narita Airport Tokyo's primary gateway; most budget flights end up here. It's 60 to 90 minutes (and around ¥3000) for an express train or bus to the city centre; buy tickets at the kiosks in the arrivals terminal. Discount buses (¥1000) run to Tokyo Station; purchase tickets on board. Fixed-fare taxis start at ¥23,000.

Haneda Airport Tokyo's smaller, closer airport with train and monorail access (15 minutes; ¥300 to ¥500) to the city centre. Fixed-fare taxis cost around ¥7000.

HOW MUCH FOR A

Bowl of noodles
¥800

Karaoke session
¥2000

Craft beer
¥1000

GETTING AROUND

Subway and train The subway is the quickest and easiest way to get around central Tokyo. The overground Yamanote (loop) and Chuo-Sobu (central) train lines, both operated by East Japan Railway Company (JR East), also service major stations. Both run from 5am to midnight. Rides cost ¥170 to ¥320. Purchase prepaid fare cards (Suica or Pasmo) from one of the ticket vending machines.

Taxi Fares start at ¥420 for the first 1km, then rise by ¥80 for every 233m you travel. There's a surcharge of 20% between 10pm and 5am. Credit cards accepted.

Walking Subway stations are close in the city centre; save yen and see more by walking if you only need to go one stop.

WHEN TO GO

JAN–MAR
Brisk but sunny days, perfect for winter sports

APR–JUN
Warm days – a popular time to visit

JUL–SEP
Rainy season; hot and humid days with typhoons

OCT–DEC
The tail end of hiking season, with cooler weather

EATING & DRINKING

Tokyo's dining scene careens nonchalantly between highs and lows: with top-class sushi restaurants and oil-spattered noodle joints earning similar accolades. There's very little you can't get here, but the one truly Tokyo dish is *nigiri-zushi* (hand-pressed sushi). Every neighbourhood has at least one sushi shop, with set meals from ¥2500. Tokyo's trendiest restaurants take the neo-bistro format, blending Japanese and international influences; look for them in Harajuku, Aoyama, Tomigaya, Ebisu and Meguro. Reservations are recommended for mid- to high-end restaurants.

Best craft cocktails
SG Club (p62)

Must-try ramen
Mensho (p61)

CONNECT & FIND YOUR WAY

Wi-fi There are plenty of free hotspots, though connection can be spotty. The best way to stay connected is to rent a pocket wi-fi device (at the airport) or buy a SIM card (data-only; at the airport or electronics stores).

Navigation Tokyo's address system is challenging, even for locals. All the more reason to have stable wi-fi, so you can rely on navigation apps.

DISCOUNT TRAVEL CARD

Tokyo Subway Ticket Gives unlimited rides on all subway lines (24/48/72hr ¥800/1200/1500; half-price for children), but not JR lines. See www.tokyometro.jp.

WHERE TO STAY

Tokyo is pricey, but there are plenty of attractive budget and midrange options. Pick somewhere near where you plan to spend the most time.

Neighbourhood	Pro/Con
Shinjuku	Major transit hub. Widest range of options at all price points. Major crowds.
Shibuya	Nightlife at your door and big-city buzz (also a downside). Good transit links.
Roppongi	Art museums and nightlife. Noisy with less convenient outer areas.
Ginza	Central with great shopping and dining. Congested and pricey.
Ueno & Yanaka	Easy airport access and good value. Yanaka has a local feel; quiet at night.
Asakusa	Best budget options. Quiet at night, with a long commute to west-side sights.

MONEY

Carry a few thousand yen in cash as some shops and restaurants don't take cards. **Tokyo Cheapo** (tokyocheapo.com) has budget tips.

01 The Definitive
TOKYO SHRINE

CULTURE | ARCHITECTURE | GARDENS

Meiji-jingu (Meiji Shrine) is Tokyo's signature Shinto shrine. It's a major tourist attraction but is also appreciated by locals: it is set in a 70-hectare forest that literally offers a breath of fresh air even though it's right in the thick of the city. A shrine visit is also a great way to participate in Japanese culture.

UING/SHUTTERSTOCK ©

📍 How to

Getting here The JR Yamanote line to Harajuku Station (west exit) or the Chiyoda line to Meiji-jingumae (exit 2).

When to go As early as possible! The shrine is least crowded in the morning. It's open dawn until dusk, which can be rather early in Tokyo, especially in winter.

Cost Free!

Photo op The colourful sake barrels (gifted to the shrine from sake makers – sake and Shinto have a long connection).

MATT MUNRO/LONELY PLANET ©

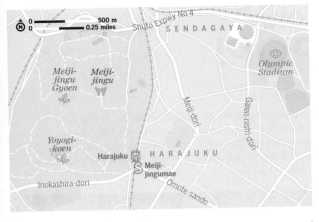

Left *Torii*, Meiji-jingu.
Below Sake barrels, Meiji-jingu.

🏯 Way of the Gods

Shinto, or 'the way of the gods', is the oldest existent belief system in Japan. Its innumerable *kami* (gods) are located mostly in nature (in trees, rocks, waterfalls and mountains, for example), but also in the objects of daily life, like hearths and wells. Historically, extraordinary people could be recognised as *kami* upon death, such as the Emperor Meiji (1852–1912) who, along with his wife, is enshrined at Meiji-jingu.

Emperor Meiji's reign coincided with Japan's transformation from isolationist, feudal state to modern nation. But that doesn't mean visitors are here to worship the former emperor. People visit for all kinds of reasons: to pray for luck in love, business, or exams; to connect with their culture; or to take a moment out of their daily lives.

Pass through the gates The shrine is at the end of a long (700m) gravel path. Along the way, you'll pass under three towering, wooden *torii* (shrine gates). These mark the boundary between the mundane world and the sacred world, and you'll see locals bowing here before passing through.

Purify yourself at the font Before the final *torii* is the *temizu-ya* (font), where it is the custom to purify yourself: dip the ladle in the water and first rinse your left hand then your right. Pour some water into your left hand and rinse your mouth, then rinse your left hand again. Make sure none of this water gets back into the font!

Make an offering In front of the main shrine building, with its cypress beams and copper-plated roof, there's a box for offerings. To make one (along with a wish), toss a coin – a ¥5 coin is considered lucky – into the box, bow twice, clap your hands twice and then bow again. (Note that you can't take photos here, or anywhere where there is a roof over your head.)

Relax in the gardens Most visitors bypass Meiji-jingu Gyoen, the garden on the shrine grounds (¥500 admission), which means it's usually quiet. It has all the elements of a classic Japanese stroll garden, with a pond and seasonal blooms – it's particularly famous for its irises in June.

02 Tokyo POP!

POP CULTURE | CITY LIFE | SHOPPING

From Godzilla to the animated films of Miyazaki Hayao, Hello Kitty to Pokémon, Japanese pop culture has captivated the world for generations. Tokyo offers many ways to engage with your favourite characters and immerse yourself in their fantasy worlds. (And if you're not already a fan of Japanese pop culture, the city might just turn you into one.)

CRIS FOTO/SHUTTERSTOCK ©

📔 How to

Tips Admission to the Ghibli Museum, Mitaka is limited and tickets go fast; see the website (ghibli-museum. jp) for details on how to purchase, and plan months in advance. Akihabara's main street, Chuo-dori, is closed to cars on Sunday afternoons, making this the best (and most popular) time to visit.

Photo-ops The light-up, true-to-size **Unicorn Gundam** (p46) in Odaiba and the **Godzilla statue** (p47) in Shinjuku.

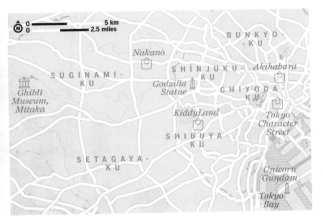

Left Akihabara district.
Below Retro toys, Mandrake Complex.

Ghibli Museum, Mitaka Studio Ghibli, which was co-founded by directors Miyazaki Hayao and Takahata Isao, is consistently responsible for Japan's most critically acclaimed and commercially successful animated films – a rare combination. It's also responsible for turning out a whole generation of Japanophiles – those who fell in love with films like *Nausicaä of the Valley of the Wind* (1984), *My Neighbor Totoro* (1988) and *Spirited Away* (2001).

The museum captures the spirit of wonder that makes the films so enchanting, and several beloved characters are worked into the design. It's equally fun for adults and kids. There's also a small cinema here that screens original shorts directed by Miyazaki, Takahata and their protégés. Check the website for regular updates on what's available. Naturally, the museum has an excellent gift shop.

Akihabara ('Akiba') Tokyo's famous pop-culture district, filled with shops selling anime (Japanese animation), manga (Japanese comics) and gaming merch, neon-bright electronics stores, retro arcades, cosplay cafes, and *gashapon* (capsule toy vending machines). From Akihabara Station, take the Electric Town exit.

Nakano Less flash and bling than Akiba. The highlight here is **Nakano Broadway**, a vintage 1960s shopping mall and home to the original **Mandarake Complex** – the go-to store for all things manga and anime. (There are other branches, including one in Akiba, but the one in Nakano, spread out over 25 tiny, niche shops, is the best.)

Cute Characters

Where to shop for your (or your kids') favourite characters:

Kiddyland Multistorey toy emporium in Harajuku that has all the Sanrio (of Hello Kitty fame) characters covered, plus Studio Ghibli, and more.

Pokémon Center Mega Tokyo Japan's largest official Pokémon shop sells every piece of the series' merchandise. Inside the Sunshine City mall in Ikebukuro.

Tokyo Character Street Over a dozen small (and often changing) shops covering a variety of characters (from Ultraman to Pretty Cure). Inside Tokyo Station.

Godzilla Store Tokyo Posters, figures, T-shirts and more. In Shinjuku.

Tokyo
ICONS

01 Hachiko

Tokyo's most famous loyal dog, who showed up daily to meet his master at Shibuya Station long after the man's death, commemorated as a statue.

02 Tokyo Tower

Eiffel Tower-like in design, this 1958 broadcast tower symbolised Tokyo's rise from the ashes after WWII.

03 Asahi Flame

The Philippe Starck-designed headquarters for Asahi Beer in Asakusa is nicknamed the 'golden turd'.

04 Unicorn Gundam

A 19.7m-tall model of an RX-0 Unicorn Gundam from the wildly popular *Mobile Suit Gundam* anime franchise.

05 Kaminarimon

The 'Thunder Gate' at the entrance to Tokyo's oldest temple, Senso-ji, is instantly recognisable with its enormous *chochin* (lantern).

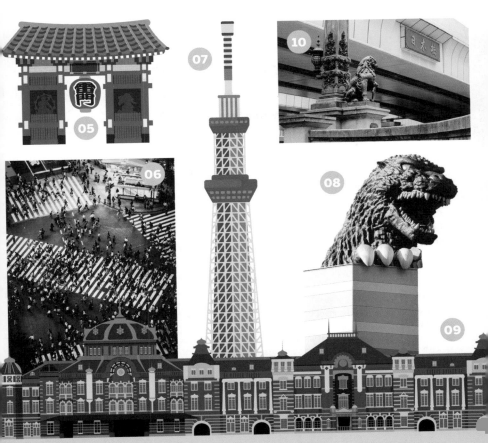

06 Shibuya Crossing

Tokyo's most photo-graphed intersection, rumoured to be the busiest in the world (and at least the busiest in Japan).

07 Tokyo Skytree

This sleek, mesh spire is Tokyo's current broadcast tower, completed in 2012 and standing 634m-tall. At night, it's illuminated in either blue or purple.

08 Shinjuku Toho Building

A 12m-tall Godzilla statue on the roof looks ready to bite into this building by Toho (the studio that produces the films).

09 Tokyo Station

Tokyo's central rail terminus, completed in 1914, was constructed when the vogue for European-style architecture was at its peak.

10 Nihombashi

This 1911 granite bridge, guarded by bronze lions and dragons, marks the geographical centre of Tokyo.

01 DFLC PRINTS/SHUTTERSTOCK ©, 02 KENJIROU MORITA/SHUTTERSTOCK ©, 03 BARKS/SHUTTERSTOCK ©, 04 BANKRX/SHUTTERSTOCK ©, 05 KENJIROU MORITA/SHUTTERSTOCK ©, 06 JONATHAN STOKES/LONELY PLANET ©, 07 BARKS/SHUTTERSTOCK ©, 08 ANDY SHIH/SHUTTERSTOCK ©, 09 SHRIKEE/SHUTTERSTOCK ©, 10 NED SNOWMAN/SHUTTERSTOCK ©

03 Hidden Dining ALLEYS

FOOD | DRINK | CITY LIFE

Scattered around Tokyo, often in the shadow of train tracks or wedged among skyscrapers, are clusters of alleys that house bars and restaurants so small they might not seat a dozen, sometimes with makeshift outdoor seating (folding tables and turned-over beer crates) tacked on. Tokyoites love them and odds are you will, too.

🗺 How to

When to go Early (around 5pm or 6pm) to grab a seat at popular places, or later in the evening, after 9pm. This is especially the case if you're a group (as space is limited); solo travellers (and sometimes pairs) can generally show up whenever and trust that space will be made.

Cost Many spots will charge a service fee (¥300 to ¥1000 per person); this is always the case if you're given a free appetizer.

Yokocho The word *yokocho* means 'side town' and is often used to describe these clusters of eating and drinking alleys. Many began as black markets after WWII, and still occupy the same hastily constructed wooden buildings. It's this look and feel of an otherwise long-gone Tokyo that endears them to locals. Note that it's considered bad form to linger past your last order, unless you're a regular customer.

Omoide-yokocho Tokyo's most famous (and photographed) *yokocho*, near Shinjuku Station. Many shops here specialise in *yakitori* (meats or vegetables

Right above Street restaurant, Omoide-yokocho.
Right below *Yakitori*, Omoide-yokocho.

🔪 Yakitori

Yakitori is a *yokocho* staple, and *yakitori* restaurants can often be identified by their red *chochin* (lanterns) hanging outside. You can order tasting sets (*moriawase*) or 'by the skewer', seasoned with salt (*shio*) or sauce (*tare*). Sit at the counter and watch the grill masters at work.

grilled on skewers). Several have English menus, and open entrances mean you can easily see inside.

Ebisu-yokocho A covered shopping arcade refitted as an eating and drinking strip. There's a wider range of food on offer here than at Omoide-yokocho (and the quality is a bit higher), including seafood (grilled or served as sashimi). English menus are scarce but you can get a sense of what to order by seeing what everyone else is eating. Gets packed; in Ebisu.

Nonbei-yokocho Two lanes of bars, bistros and *izakaya* (Japanese pub-eateries) along-side Shibuya's elevated train tracks. You'll need some courage to open the doors as there's little indication of what to expect from outside.

04 Samurai Swords & **SILK KIMONOS**

CULTURE | ARTS | HISTORY

The Tokyo National Museum houses the world's largest collection of Japanese art, including ancient pottery, Buddhist sculptures, samurai swords, colourful *ukiyo-e* (woodblock prints), gorgeous kimonos and much, much more. It's organised so that visitors can easily take in the greatest hits – in a couple of hours.

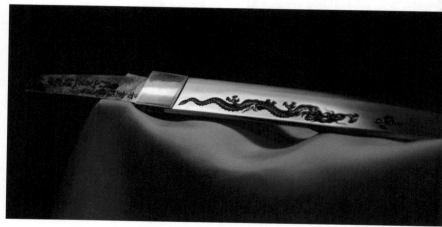

NANO CALVO/ALAMY STOCK PHOTO ©

🗺 **How to**

Getting here The Tokyo National Museum is a short walk from Ueno Station (Ueno-koen exit).

When to go The permanent collection is usually uncrowded. For a couple of weeks in spring and autumn, the back garden, home to five vintage teahouses, opens to the public.

Cost ¥1000 (student/child ¥500/free)

Tips Use the lockers (¥100 deposit) for your bag or coat and pick up a free copy of the brochure *Highlights of Japanese Art,* which explains everything in English.

FREDERIC SOREAU/ALAMY STOCK PHOTO ©

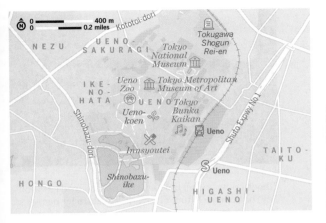

Above Samurai sword, Tokyo National Musuem.
Below Edo-period kimono, Tokyo National Museum.

The Japanese Gallery The museum is divided into several buildings. Buy your ticket from outside the main gate, then head straight for the structure with the sloping tiled roof at the back, the Honkan, which houses the Japanese Gallery. Take the central staircase up to the 2nd floor, where the exhibitions are arranged chronologically, starting with prehistoric pottery.

You'll pass through rooms featuring Buddhist mandala paintings, ink brush scrolls, and tea ceremony pottery before reaching rooms 5 and 6. Here, glistening **swords**, lacquer-plate armour and dramatic helmets – with mounted ornaments and face guards designed to terrify – bring the samurai to life. The samurai were iconic warriors of Japan's medieval age, spanning the 12th to 19th centuries, and some of the swords on display are old indeed. If you're travelling with kids, these rooms are sure to impress.

Another highlight is room 10, which features art of the Edo period (1603–1868), including colourful *ukiyo-e* and sumptuous **kimonos** worn by the nobility and actors on the stage. The decorative motifs – painstakingly embroidered by hand – on kimonos are highly seasonal: pine needles for winter or cherry blossoms for spring, for example, and the kimonos on display reflect this.

The Gallery of Horyu-ji Treasures Spare another half hour to visit this enchanting gallery, which displays masks, scrolls and gilt Buddhas from Horyu-ji (in Nara Prefecture, dating from 607). It's housed in an elegant, box-shaped contemporary building (1999) by Taniguchi Yoshio.

TOKYO EXPERIENCES

🚶 Stetch Your Legs

The Tokyo National Museum is part of sprawling Ueno-koen (Ueno Park). It doesn't have lawns, but there are strolling paths, which make this a good place to stretch your legs (or let the kids run around). Within the grounds are shrines, temples, Tokyo's zoo and a pond, **Shinobazu-ike**, full of lotuses that bloom in July.

In the main plaza, there's a Starbucks with lots of patio seating. Towards the pond is **Innsyoutei** (innsyoutei. jp), a gorgeous wooden teahouse dating to 1875 serving classic Japanese cuisine either as a course or as a *bento* (boxed meal). It's a wonderful spot for lunch; reservations recommended. There are also usually food stalls by the pond.

Singing All the Songs

SING THE NIGHT AWAY, JAPAN-STYLE

Karaoke isn't just about singing: it's an excuse to let loose, bond, and keep the party going into the early hours. It's a way to express yourself – are you the type to sing the latest pop hit (dance moves included) or do you go all in on an emotional ballad?

Trends come and go but karaoke (pronounced ka-ra-oh-kay) has been a fixture of Japanese culture for decades. It doesn't matter if you're a good singer or not, as long as you've got heart.

In Japan, karaoke is usually sung in private rooms with friends, at establishments called karaoke boxes. A typical karaoke box has multiple floors with dozens of rooms of varying sizes. All major cities have them, in entertainment districts or around major train stations. Smaller cities often have one near the main train station, and it just might be the only after-dark entertainment option around.

Karaoke Basics

You enter a karaoke box as you do a hotel, heading first to the counter in the lobby. Reservations aren't required, though occasionally you may have to wait for a room to open up. Some chains may require a nominal membership, which someone in the group will have to sign up for (so make sure at least one person has ID on them). Otherwise, the first step is to tell the staff the size of your party.

Then you need to work out for how long you want to rent a room. Most places charge admission per person per 30 minutes, with a one-hour minimum. If you're not sure how long you want to commit, you can book the initial one hour and then choose to extend by 30 minutes or an hour indefinitely (so long as no one is waiting on an empty room and it's not yet closing time). Pricing varies by day and time of day, being most expensive on

Left Karaoke microphone.
Centre Big Echo, Maruonuchi branch.
Right Karaoke performance.

Friday and Saturday nights (around ¥500 per 30 minutes) and cheapest on weekend afternoons (around ¥150 per 30 minutes).

Alternatively, most establishments offer various packages, which may include unlimited drinks (*nomihodai*) and/or room rental for a set number of hours (often called 'free time'). These packages are usually a much better deal than ordering drinks and food à la carte and paying by the hour.

> It doesn't matter if you're a good singer or not, as long as you've got heart.

When you're inside your room, locate the console, which you'll use to select songs. In most chains, it's possible to switch the console into English and search songs alphabetically. If there's no English function, check the room (or ask staff) for a songbook – a huge paper directory of all the songs – that will list English-language songs in English (you enter the song code into the console). English songs will play with the lyrics in English on the screen.

Pro tip: Queue up several songs so that you don't waste precious karaoke time mulling over what to sing next.

You can order food and drink via the telephone in the room. Staff will ring you around 10 minutes before your session is due to expire; you can extend or decide to call it a night. When your time is up, return to the lobby (taking the tab with you if there's one in the room) to pay.

☆ Karaoke Boxes

Karaoke boxes are easy to spot: just look for the colourful, illuminated signs spelling out カラオケ (karaoke). Most are chains, and it's these that have the biggest songbooks, offer non-smoking rooms, and are most likely to have consoles and menus in English.

Big Echo (ビッグエコー; big-echo.jp) The biggest national chain and all-round good option.

Karaoke-kan (カラオケ館; karaokekan.jp) Ubiquitous, nationwide and cheap.

Uta Hiroba (歌広場; utahiro. com) Tokyo area, free soft drinks; look for the smiley face logo.

Jankara (ジャンカラ; jankara.ne.jp) Kansai area (Kyoto, Osaka, Nara etc) and Kyushu; cheap all-you-can-drink packages.

05 Shopping SPREE

FASHION | ART | FOOD

▬▬▬ Tokyo is a fantastic place to shop. It's the most fashion-forward of all Japanese cities, but it also has a strong artisan tradition, which means you can get that one-of-a-kind piece of clothing as well as a finely honed chef's knife (and, really, just about anything).

PICTURE CELLS/SHUTTERSTOCK ©

🗺 How to

Duty-free Department stores, chain stores and, increasingly, boutiques offer duty-free shopping – make sure you have your passport handy. Tax is taken off at the register or, in larger stores, refunded at a designated counter.

Fitting rooms Take your shoes off inside and use the white, disposable face cover when trying on tops.

Opening hours Major shops are open seven days a week; smaller boutiques usually have one or two days off midweek. Many boutiques don't open until 11am or noon.

CHIKAKO NOBUHARA/GETTY IMAGES ©

Fashion Districts

Ginza Tokyo's classic, central shopping district, anchored by famous department stores like **Mitsukoshi**. There are also some new high-end malls that carry a mix of Japanese and international brands. The best is **Ginza Six**, which is worth a visit for its art installations in the atrium. Nearest station: Ginza.

Harajuku West-side neighbourhood and internationally famous shopping destination. Many well-known Japanese fashion labels (like **COMME des GARÇONS**) have their flagship stores here, or in neighbouring **Aoyama**. Dig deep into the side streets (on either side of the boulevard, Omote-sando) to discover the ever-changing, tiny boutiques and second-hand stores from which Harajuku hipsters cobble together their head-turning

JONLU/SHUTTERSTOCK ©

🛍 Flea Markets

Tokyo's best market, with hundreds of vendors, is the twice-monthly **Oedo Antique Market**, in the courtyard of the Tokyo International Forum. Most weekends there is a flea or craft market at **Commune**, a trendy indoor-outdoor space in Aoyama.

Above left Ginza Six shopping complex.
Above right Tax-free shopping.
Left Oedo Antique Market.

looks. Convenient stations: Harajuku, Meiji-jingumae and Omote-sando.

Shibuya Major commercial district with malls and department stores, including **Shibuya Parco**. Shibuya is adjacent to Harajuku – it's not really clear where one ends and the other begins; pedestrian **Cat Street**, which connects the two, has lots of boutiques. Nearest station: Shibuya.

Daikanyama Many smaller and up-and-coming Japanese brands have boutiques in this low-key fashionable neighbourhood that is otherwise largely residential. Most shops are within the wedge formed by the intersection of Hachiman-dori and Kyu-Yamate-dori, a short walk from the central exit of Daikanyama Station (one stop from Shibuya on the Tokyu Toyoko line).

Arts & Crafts

In Tokyo, you can find locally made crafts and also regional crafts from around Japan, including pottery, lacquerware, glasswork

🛍 Best for...

Japanese designers
Shinjuku department store **Isetan** carries both established and up-and-coming Japanese fashion labels for men and women.

Traditional arts and crafts Part showroom, part shop **Japan Traditional Crafts Aoyama Square** stocks heirloom pieces, but also beautiful items at reasonable prices.

Kitchen and gourmet
Pick up artisan foodstuffs and homewares at **Akomeya**; branches in Shinjuku and Ginza.

Souvenirs Emporium of miscellany **Tokyu Hands** is full of fascinating things you didn't know you wanted; branches in Shinjuku and Shibuya.

Stationery and art In Ginza, **Itoya** stocks quality paper goods for everyday use or special occasions.

Left Tokyu Hands department store.
Below Colourful bowls, Kappabashi-dori

and cast-iron teapots. Major **department stores** (such as Isetan, Mitsukoshi and Takashimaya) carry works by contemporary artisans on their homewares floors.

Older neighbourhoods on the east side of the city, like **Asakusa**, have some fantastic shops, some of them centuries-old and still run by the same families. The area around the temple, Senso-ji, is a good place to start (nearest station: Asakusa). Many newer artisans have set up shop in **Kuramae**, a former warehouse district just south of Asakusa (walk or take the Toei Asakusa line one stop to Kuramae).

Speciality Districts

Kappabashi-dori Tokyo's restaurant supply district. While it's set up for pros, many shops have stuff (like bamboo steamer baskets and lacquer bowls for miso soup) for home cooks, too. Excellent knife store **Kama-asa** is here. Nearest station: Tawaramachi (but also a short walk from Asakusa).

Jinbocho The second-hand bookshops district is in central Tokyo, along Yasukuni-dori. Most titles are in Japanese, but there are also some shops specialising in art books, like **Komiyama Shoten**, and also vintage maps and *ukiyo-e*, like **Ohya Shobo**. There are also lots of great coffee shops here. Nearest station: Jinbocho.

06 An Afternoon in YANAKA

WALKING | ART | ARCHITECTURE

Yanaka is the rare Tokyo neighbourhood that still has a high concentration of old wooden buildings, as well as small, quiet temples, winding alleys, galleries and ateliers. It's popular with locals and visitors alike, who come to soak up the old-Tokyo atmosphere.

KUREMO/SHUTTERSTOCK ©

🗺 Trip Notes

Getting here Chiyoda subway line stops Nezu (start) and Sendagi (finish) are the most convenient.

Getting around Yanaka is ideal for walking.

When to go Weekends can get a little congested, though note weekday closings of some sights.

Top tip Yanaka is also a short walk from the Tokyo National Museum; spend the morning at the museum and the afternoon exploring Yanaka.

☕ Take a Break

Yanaka has some wonderful cafes, like **Kayaba Coffee**, which has been serving coffee and sandwiches since the 1930s. **Yanaka Beer Hall** has craft beer on tap; it's in a lightly renovated old wooden building, with outdoor seating. On a hot day, get shaved ice from ever-popular **Himitsu-do** (look for the queue).

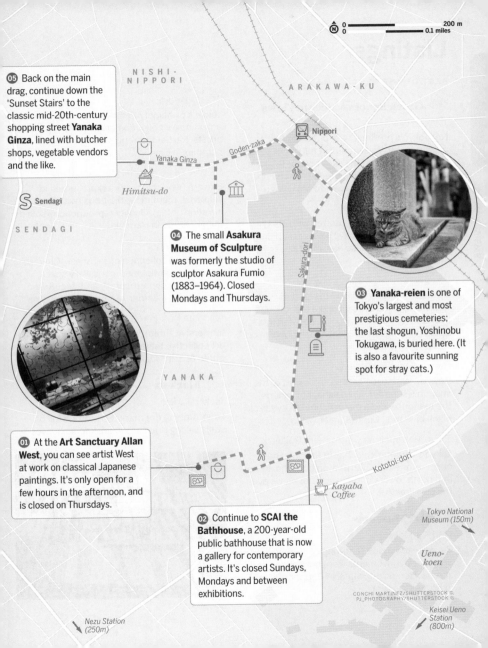

05 Back on the main drag, continue down the 'Sunset Stairs' to the classic mid-20th-century shopping street **Yanaka Ginza**, lined with butcher shops, vegetable vendors and the like.

NISHI-NIPPORI

ARAKAWA-KU

Nippori

Goden-zaka

Yanaka Ginza

Himitsu-do

S Sendagi

SENDAGI

04 The small **Asakura Museum of Sculpture** was formerly the studio of sculptor Asakura Fumio (1883–1964). Closed Mondays and Thursdays.

Sakura-dori

03 **Yanaka-reien** is one of Tokyo's largest and most prestigious cemeteries; the last shogun, Yoshinobu Tokugawa, is buried here. (It is also a favourite sunning spot for stray cats.)

YANAKA

01 At the **Art Sanctuary Allan West**, you can see artist West at work on classical Japanese paintings. It's only open for a few hours in the afternoon, and is closed on Thursdays.

Kototoi-dori

Kayaba Coffee

02 Continue to **SCAI the Bathhouse**, a 200-year-old public bathhouse that is now a gallery for contemporary artists. It's closed Sundays, Mondays and between exhibitions.

Tokyo National Museum (150m)

Ueno-koen

CONCHI MARTINEZ/SHUTTERSTOCK ©, PJ_PHOTOGRAPHY/SHUTTERSTOCK ©

Nezu Station (250m)

Keisei Ueno Station (800m)

Listings

BEST OF THE REST

🌿 Green Spaces & Scenic Views

Yoyogi-koen

Not Tokyo's prettiest park but definitely its most popular. Weekends are full of picnickers, Frisbee games and the like; look for festivals at the plaza across the street. Free and open 24/7. In Harajuku, adjacent to Meiji-jingu.

Shinjuku-gyoen

With manicured lawns (dotted with cherry trees) this is one of Tokyo's classiest picnic spots. The greenhouse has spectacular orchids. In Shinjuku.

Rikugi-en

An elegant stroll garden with wooded walkways, stone bridges and a teahouse overlooking the central pond. Located in a quiet, north Tokyo residential neighbourhood, and rarely crowded.

Hama-rikyu Onshi-teien

Bayside landscape garden, once part of the shogun's summer villa. Highlights include the teahouse and a magnificent 300-year-old black pine tree. Central (near Ginza).

Tokyo Metropolitan Government Building

Tokyo's landmark city hall in Shinjuku has observatories (at 202m) atop both the south and north towers of Building 1, for views over the city. Free!

🖼 Art Museums

Mori Art Museum

Blockbuster shows featuring contemporary artists and movements from both Japan and abroad. Bonus: open late. In Roppongi (part of Roppongi Hills).

TOP Museum

Tokyo's principal photography museum, with an extensive collection of works by Japanese artists. Part of the Yebisu Garden Place complex in Ebisu.

Ukiyo-e Ota Memorial Museum of Art

Ukiyo-e (woodblock prints) presented in seasonal, thematic exhibitions (with English curation notes). Quality reproductions sold in the gift store. In Harajuku.

Nezu Museum

A renowned collection of Japanese, Chinese and Korean antiquities in a gallery space designed by contemporary architect Kuma Kengo (with a garden out back). In Aoyama.

teamLab Borderless

Immersive, interactive experience from digital art collective teamLab. Fun for kids and full of photo ops. In Odaiba; book tickets online.

🛍 Markets

Tsukiji Market

Long-running dry market crammed full of stalls selling dried seaweed, kitchen knives

Tsukiji Market.

LERNER VADIM/SHUTTERSTOCK ©

and more. Food stalls, too. Only open in the mornings; near Ginza.

Toyosu Market

Tokyo's central wholesale market, where the famous tuna auction is held most mornings. Check the website for access instructions. Tokyo Bay area.

Ameya-yokocho

Old-school, open-air market (originally a post-WWII black market) with vendors selling everything from fresh seafood to vintage jeans. In Ueno.

Ameya-yokocho.

Sushi & Classic Japanese

Tonki ¥

Tokyo *tonkatsu* (crumbed pork cutlet) institution for over 80 years. In Meguro; English menu.

Sushi Dai ¥¥

The classic spot for sushi breakfast at the fish market. Note: this is at the market in Toyosu, not Tsukiji. Come very early or expect to queue.

Sahsya Kanetanaka ¥¥

Approachable *kaiseki* (Japanese haute cuisine): elegant lunch sets of seasonal delicacies, with longer courses for dinner (reservations required). In Harajuku; English menu.

Tensuke ¥¥

Popular local tempura spot, famous for its egg tempura that's batter-crisp on the outside and runny in the middle. Expect to queue; in Koenji (west of Shinjuku).

sushi m ¥¥¥

Creative sushi paired with boutique wines and sake (including some truly rare bottles). A memorable splurge, in Aoyama. Booking essential; English menu.

Izakaya, Bistros & Gastronomy

Shinsuke ¥¥

Nearly 100-years-old *izakaya* (Japanese pub-eatery) with a long cedar counter, seasonal menu and premium sake. In Ueno. Reservations recommended; English menu.

Narukiyo ¥¥¥

Local favourite *izakaya*, serving excellent renditions of all the classics with a side order of punk-rock cheek. In Aoyama. Reservations recommended.

Kabi ¥¥¥

Japanese-meets-Nordic cuisine with an emphasis on fermented ingredients, paired with natural wines and sakes. In Meguro. Reservations required; English menu.

Eatrip ¥¥¥

Major player in Tokyo's farm-to-table movement, serving Japanese dishes with international inflections in a wooden house on a Harajuku side street. Reservations recommended; English menu.

Noodles & Sandwiches

Mensho ¥

The Tokyo ramen darling of the moment. Branches near Tokyo Dome City (Kasuga

KORKUSUNG/SHUTTERSTOCK ©

Station) and in Shibuya (inside Shibuya Parco); vegan options in Shibuya. English menu.

Afuri ¥

Afuri's specialty is *yuzu-shio* ramen (a light, salty broth flavoured with *yuzu,* a type of citrus). Branches around town, but the original is in Ebisu. English menu.

Delifucious ¥

Deluxe fish burgers dreamed up by a former sushi chef. In Shibuya (inside Shibuya Parco). English menu.

☕ Coffee & Tea

Turret Coffee ¥

Tokyo's best latte (get the Turret latte), in Tsukiji. Named for the three-wheeled trucks that used to cruise around the old Tsukiji Market (there's one in the shop).

Fuglen Tokyo ¥

Local hotspot with a cool mid-20th-century Scandi decor and perfect pours of the cafe's signature light-roast, single-origin beans. In Tomigaya (near Shibuya).

Sakurai Japanese Tea Experience ¥¥

Tasting courses that pair different styles and regions of Japanese tea with traditional sweets; reserve for courses. In Aoyama.

🍸 Drinks with a View

Two Rooms ¥¥

Tokyo's best terrace, overlooking Harajuku. Call ahead (staff speak English) to reserve a Friday or Saturday night spot under the stars.

New York Bar ¥¥¥

The definitive high-altitude Tokyo night spot, on the 52nd floor of the Park Hyatt in Shinjuku, with sweeping views from the floor-to-ceiling windows.

🍺 Craft Beer, Sake & Cocktails

Mikkeller Tokyo ¥¥

Beers from pioneer 'gypsy brewer' Mikkel Borg Bjergsø. In the side streets of Shibuya.

Another 8 ¥¥

Japanese craft beer and small-batch sake in a renovated garage in Meguro. Live DJs on most Friday and Saturday evenings.

Gem by Moto ¥¥

Gem specialises in boutique sakes. Bookings recommended; in Ebisu.

SG Club ¥¥¥

Creative cocktails in Shibuya from award-winning bartender Shingo Gokan. Reserve a seat in the speakeasy-like basement.

🛍 Home & Kitchen

Kama-asa

The place to get hand-forged kitchen knives, plus cast-iron cooking ware. Near Asakusa.

Imadeya

Small but mighty wine and liquor shop, with an excellent selection of sake and other made-in-Japan spirits. In the basement of Ginza Six mall.

WORLD DISCOVERY/ALAMY STOCK PHOTO ©

COMME des GARÇONS.

d47 design travel store

Showcase for exceptional regional Japanese artisanship from trendy lifestyle brand D&D Department. In Shibuya.

🛍 Fashion & Vintage

Beams Japan

Several floors of curated Japanese fashion brands, plus original artwork and contemporary crafts. In Shinjuku.

Okura

Contemporary T-shirts and hoodies and also items that riff on older silhouettes, like the trailing sleeves of a kimono, all dyed with indigo. In Daikanyama.

COMME des GARÇONS

Flagship store for designer Kawakubo Rei's ground-breaking label, COMME des GARÇONS. In Aoyama.

Pass the Baton

Personal castaways (including vintage designer pieces) and dead stock from long-defunct retailers. In Harajuku (in the basement of Omotesando Hills).

House @Mikiri Hassin

Hidden deep in the side alleys of Harajuku, House stocks an ever-changing selection of experimental Japanese fashion brands. Look for 'ハウス' spelled vertically in neon.

RagTag

This consignment shop is stocked with labels loved by Harajuku shoppers: Vivienne Westwood, Junya Watanabe and more.

🛍 Malls & Department Stores

Shibuya Parco

Trend-setting department store with international and Japanese brands, plus pop-ups and trunk shows from under-the-radar designers.

Coredo Muromachi.

PICTURE CELLS/SHUTTERSTOCK ©

Coredo Muromachi

Spread over several buildings, with a focus on homewares and gourmet shops. In Nihombashi, one of Tokyo's oldest neighbourhoods.

Ginza Six

High-end mall with art installations and a branch of Tsutaya Books (with many art, design and travel titles in English).

Mitsukoshi

Classic Ginza department store, with an excellent homewares floor and basement gourmet food hall.

♨ Onsen & Spas

Spa LaQua

Huge spa complex with indoor and outdoor baths fed by natural hot springs plus a variety of saunas. Part of the Tokyo Dome City complex in central Tokyo (Suidobashi Station).

Kamata Onsen

Old-school public bathhouse famous for its mineral-rich black water, courtesy of underground springs seeped in volcanic ash. In Kamata, a suburb south of Tokyo.

Scan for more things to see, do and try in Tokyo

07 Day Trip to **NIKKO**

CULTURE | ADVENTURE | AUTUMN

An unforgettable autumn getaway awaits a mere two-hour train ride from Tokyo. The historic town of Nikko and neighbouring Kinugawa Onsen are among the best places to view the autumn foliage in the Kanto region, and whether you're looking for culture, action or relaxation, there's plenty to experience. Here's where to begin.

🗺 How to

Getting here The Tobu Nikko line connects central Tokyo's Asakusa Station directly to Nikko and Kinugawa Onsen.

When to go Autumn leaves in this area are at their peak in early November.

How much Tobu Railway (tobu.co.jp/foreign) offers a variety of travel passes from ¥2040. A night at a ryokan starts from ¥10,000 per person.

Afternoon snack Pop by Nikko Sakaeya near Tobu Nikko Station for *ageyuba manju,* a local fried delicacy.

Pick Your Path

Worship Set against the backdrop of a lush forest, **Tosho-gu** is the final resting place of Tokugawa Ieyasu, founder of the Tokugawa shogunate. This Shinto shrine is one of the most elaborate and beautiful in the country and features the best traditional architecture and artisanship.

Nature's wonders Kegon-no-taki is a sight to behold. An hour away by bus from Nikko Station, visitors can stand on a platform and witness one of Japan's three most beautiful waterfalls cascade 97m from a lake

Above Tosho-gu shrine.
Below Kegon-no-taki.

🔭 Shin-kyo

In Nikko, look out for a red arched footbridge extending from the main road toward a forested area. Known as **Shin-kyo** ('sacred bridge') and said to have existed prior to 1636, this Nikko landmark is among the finest bridges in Japan. Snap some photos, or make a trip across and back for a small fee (¥500).

down to the rocks below. Surrounding trees paint the area a different colour each season, and the waterfall freezes solid in winter.

Unwind Relax after a day of sightseeing and trekking at **Kinugawa Onsen**, a hot-springs town near Nikko. Flowing through the centre of town is the long, rocky Kinu-gawa, flanked by hotels and ryokan. Take a dip in the natural hot springs, and enjoy a *kaiseki* (Japanese haute cuisine) course dinner with exceptional service.

Set sail Kinugawa Line Kudari (linekudari.com) offers boat tours, where you'll strap on a safety vest and hop on to a long wooden boat for a drift down the Kinu-gawa. High above are colourful forests and jagged cliffs. The river itself is mostly calm, but sometimes choppy, so you're truly in for an exciting ride.

CHRISTOPH KT BARON MORIYAMA, DK PHOTOGRAPHY

FUJI FIVE LAKES

HIKING | NATURE | CULTURE

Experience
Fuji Five
Lakes
online

- **Trip Builder** (p68)
- **Practicalities** (p69)
- **The Iconic Mountain** (p70)
- **Escape to the Lakes** (p74)
- **Listings** (p76)

APIMUMRIN/GETTY IMA

FUJI FIVE LAKES
Trip Builder

Fuji Five Lakes is a popular outdoor destination. The big draw here is Mt Fuji, which you can climb during the summer season. Year-round, look for Fuji reflected in the lakes, from atop surrounding mountains or while soaking in open-air hot springs.

Explore bookable experiences in Fuji Five Lakes online

Sample local speciality *hoto* (a hearty noodle hotpot) at **Tenka-chaya** (p77)
🕑 *2 hours*

Hike to the top of **Mitsutoge-yama** for views of Mt Fuji and Kawaguchi-ko (p75)
🕑 *½–1 day*

Kawaguchi-ko
Kawaguchi-ko

Shoji-ko

Sai-ko

Fuji-Yoshida

Ride some of Japan's most daredevil roller coasters at **Fuji-Q Highland** (p76)
🕑 *½–1 day*

Motosu-ko

Camp on the shores of serene Motosu-ko at **Koan** (p77)
🕑 *1–2 days*

Fuji-Hakone-Izu National Park

Yamanaka-ko

Learn about the history of Fuji-worship at **Togawa-ke Oshi-no-ie Restored Pilgrim's Inn** (p76)
🕑 *2 hours*

Subash...

Summit Japan's most famous peak, **Mt Fuji** (p70)
🕑 *1–2 days*

JAMOO/SHUTTERSTOCK ©, OLIVIER BRUCHEZ/ FLICKR, CREATIVE COMMONS BY-SA 2.0 ©

0 ——— 5 km
0 ——— 2.5 miles

Practicalities

ARRIVING

Kawaguchi-ko Station The main transport hub for Fuji Five Lakes, with trains and express buses to/from Tokyo (Shinjuku). In central Kawaguchi-ko.

FIND YOUR WAY

The tourist information centre next to Kawaguchi-ko Station has English-speaking staff and lots of useful information, like bus routes and hiking maps.

MONEY

Work out all the cash you'll need (and a little extra, just in case), and have it in hand, before heading to Mt Fuji.

WHERE TO STAY

Place	Pro/Con
Kawaguchi-ko	Widest selection of accommodation and amenities. Good public transport. Very developed.
Fuji-Yoshida	More town than resort, with historical sites. Removed from natural attractions.
Sai-ko & Motosu-ko	Best for lakeside camping. Inconvenient without a car.

GETTING AROUND

Train Connects Kawaguchi-ko, Fuji-Q Highland and Fuji-Yoshida (Fujisan Station).

Bus Tourist buses run on several co-lour-coded loops, departing from Kawaguchi-ko Station. Best for getting around Kawaguchi-ko (other services are infrequent).

Car The best way to explore Fuji Five Lakes, especially the more remote lakes.

TOP: HAYACHANTA/SHUTTERSTOCK ©
BOTTOM: TRAN THI HAI YEN/SHUTTERSTOCK ©

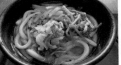

EATING & DRINKING

Kawaguchi-ko, Fuji-Yoshida and Yamanaka-ko have restaurants; if you're camping, there are several supermarkets in the area (car required).

Hoto Thick, hand-cut noodles served in a hotpot with vegetables; a Fuji Five Lakes speciality.

Yoshida udon Noodles made from wheat and barley served in a miso-spiked broth.

Best coffee with a view
Tenka-chaya (p77)

Must-try noodles
Hoto Fudo (p77)

JAN–MAR	APR–JUN	JUL–SEP	OCT–DEC
Brisk but sunny days, perfect for Fuji-spotting; chance of snow	Warm days and fresh green in the hills	Peak season for camping, water sports and climbing Mt Fuji	Popular time to visit for foliage and hiking the foothills

FUJI FIVE LAKES FIND YOUR FEET

08 The Iconic
MOUNTAIN

HIKING | NATURE | CULTURE

Mt Fuji (3776m) is Japan's tallest mountain, a perfectly formed volcanic cone rising above the clouds, and historically an object of worship. Climbing it is a summer rite of passage, something most Japanese feel they should do once in their lifetime.

🗺️ How to

Cost A ¥1000 donation per climber is requested to cover maintenance.

Resources Check news and weather updates (fujisan-climb.jp). Attempting a climb in bad weather can be miserable (at best) and dangerous (at worst).

When to go The climbing season runs 1 July to 10 September; try to avoid climbing on weekends and during the mid-August Obon holiday, when trails are most crowded.

Connect Mountain huts on the Yoshida Trail have free wi-fi.

The Trails

Mt Fuji is divided into 10 'stations' from base to summit, but the main hiking trails start halfway up, at the fifth station (as far as the roads go). There are four routes: Yoshida, Subashiri, Fujinomiya and Gotemba. Of these, the Yoshida Trail, which starts from the Fuji Subaru Line 5th Station, is by far and away the most popular route, as it's the one that is most easily accessed via public transport from Tokyo. It also has the most amenities en route (toilets, first aid stations, huts from which to buy water etc), and it is also the most crowded. For this trail, allow six to eight hours to summit and three to four hours to descend.

The Subashiri Trail is famous for its *sunabashiri* ('sand run') descent from the seventh station (sunglasses and a

🥾 Trail Access

During climbing season, there are direct buses from Shinjuku Bus Terminal (2½ hours) and Kawaguchi-ko Station (one hour) to the Fuji-Subaru Line 5th Station (for the Yoshida Trail). Access for the Subashiri and Gotemba Trails is via bus from Gotemba Station; for the Fujinomiya Trail, buses run from Mishima Station.

Above left Mt Fuji and Kawaguchi-ko.
Above right Reaching the summit on the Yoshida Trail.
Left Hiking the Subashiri Trail.

scarf or bandana to protect from dust recommended). The Fujinomiya Trail is the shortest, and convenient if you're travelling from or onwards to points west (such as Kyoto). The Gotemba has the distinction of being the longest and the least crowded (with the fewest amenities).

Note that the descending trail is often different from the ascending one. The mountain is well signposted in English, though fog at the top can make it easy to miss signs.

The Climb

Most of the climb takes place above the tree line, on ground scoria ranging in hue from dark brown to a fiery red. As you get higher, the trail becomes steeper, at points requiring hikers to scramble over boulders.

Mountain Huts

Breaking up the hike with a stay in a mountain hut is highly recommended, especially to help acclimate to the altitude. Two popular

ⓘ What to Pack

Conditions can change dramatically on Mt Fuji and it can be freezing (literally) on the summit. Pack clothes appropriate for cold and wet weather; gloves can also protect your hands from sharp rocks. If you're walking at night, you'll need a headlamp. While rare, falling rocks have caused deadly accidents; free helmet rentals are available at the sixth-station Mt Fuji Safety Guidance Center on the Yoshida Trail. Huts, located at each station, sell food and water (¥500 per 500mL bottle; cash only); they also have toilets (¥200; toilet paper, but not soap, is provided) and free wi-fi. Rubbish must be taken away.

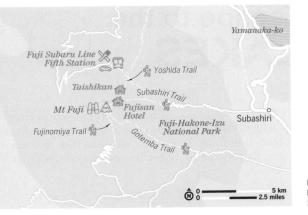

Left Sunrise at Mt Fuji's summit.
Below Mountain huts at Mt Fuji's 7th Station.

ones are **Fujisan Hotel** (fujisanhotel.com; at the Original 8th Station, where the Yoshida and Subashiri Trails meet) and **Taishikan** (mfi.or.jp/taisikan; at the lower 8th Station on the Yoshida Trail); the latter can do vegetarian and halal meals. Bookings essential.

Sunrise at the Summit

For many climbers, the goal is to see *goraiko* (the rising sun) from the summit, which happens sometime between 4.30am and 5.30am. Pre-dawn, the mountain is at its most crowded and walking slows to a crawl on the Yoshida Trail, especially above the eighth station. To account for this, you'll need to start out from the fifth station at 8pm or 9pm. Or, if you're staying at a mountain hut, depart from the eighth station around midnight or from the Original 8th Station (Hon-Hachigome) at 2am.

Still, it's often too foggy at the summit to see much. It's also cold and windy. Clearer views (with fewer crowds) are likelier from the stations below. Weather permitting, sunrise is visible from anywhere on the Yoshida Trail above the sixth station.

LEFT: NONCHANON/SHUTTERSTOCK © RIGHT: HON-CHAN/SHUTTERSTOCK ©

09 Escape to the LAKES

HIKING | NATURE | CULTURE

Fuji Five Lakes is a year-round outdoor destination. Mt Fuji looms large here, as one of the main reasons to visit is to see its perfect cone, reflected in the lakes or from surrounding mountain trails. There are also onsen (hot springs) and other natural phenomena, like lava caves, plus museums and shrines that bring the history of Fuji to life.

How to

When to go Year-round. Fuji Five Lakes is most crowded during the Golden Week holiday (late April to early May), summer season and late autumn (when the leaves change colour). In winter, snow is possible at higher elevations on some hiking trails.

Getting around If you are relying on public transport, be sure to check bus schedules in advance as some routes run infrequently.

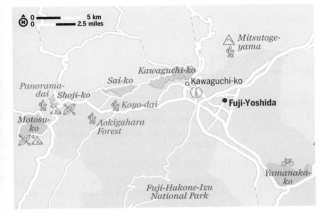

The Lakes

Kawaguchi-ko The most developed of the lakes is Kawaguch-ko. It is the easiest to reach by public transport and the best place to base yourself if you don't have a car. Many hiking trails are reachable here by bus, and there are good views of Mt Fuji from the north shore of the lake.

Sai-ko Just west of Kawaguchi-ko, is quieter and the jumping-off point for visiting caves formed by ancient lava flows, and the **Aokigahara Forest**. A flat, 3km trail through Aokigahara Forest connects two caves, Sai-ko Komoriana and Fugaku Fukestu.

Further west still is **Shoji-ko** (the smallest of the lakes) and **Motosu-ko** (the deepest). It's very quiet out this way, with just a handful of small hotels and campsites, many of which rent canoes or kayaks in the summer. While swimming is prohibited in all of the lakes, because of extremely cold temperatures just below the surface, Shoji-ko does have a small sandy beach where you can dip your toes.

The views of Mt Fuji reflected in either Shoji-ko or Motosu-ko are stunning; it's the view from Motosu-ko's northwest shore that is depicted on the back of the ¥1000 bill.

Yamanaka-ko, The largest lake is Yamanaka-ko, which is east of Kawaguchi-ko. Like Kawaguchi-ko, it has a lot of development, especially on the southern shore. One fun thing to do here is rent a bicycle and cycle the 14km bike path around the lake.

Above left Autumn colours at Sai-ko.
Below left Cycling the shores of Yamanaka-ko.

🥾 Best Hikes

Panorama-dai (1328m) A short, all-level hike (6km) with a dead-on view of Mt Fuji at the top. The trail starts at the Panorama-dai-shita bus stop, on the shore of Shoji-ko.

Koyo-dai (1165m) Half-day trek (12km) with undulating elevation change and views of Fuji, Aokigahara and Sai-ko. It's particularly recommended in late autumn, when Aoki-ga-hara's trees blaze red. Nearest bus stop: Koyo-dai-iriguchi.

Mitsutoge-yama (1785m) A local favourite hike through pretty native broadleaf forest and with views of Mt Fuji and over Kawaguchi-ko from the summit. There are a few trails, including one that picks up from the Fuji Viewing Platform, so you can tailor this one to your level.

Listings

BEST OF THE REST

⚜ Green Spaces & Scenic Views

Aokigahara Forest

This mossy, mixed-leaf forest grew atop a lava plateau that formed following a 9th-century eruption of Mt Fuji. It's very easy to get lost here, so don't stray from the trail.

Komi-koen

Grassy lawn on the banks of Kawaguchi-ko, perfect for a picnic or letting kids run around. On the southwest side of the lake.

Churei-to

This five-tiered pagoda, with Mt Fuji behind it, is a popular photo op. A short walk from Shimo-Yoshida Station.

Fuji Viewing Platform

Observation point atop Tenjo-yama (1104m) with excellent Fuji views. Access is via the Mt Fuji Panoramic Ropeway or the Mt Tenjo hiking trail (two to three hours round-trip). In Kawaguchi-ko.

♨ Museums & Shrines

Togawa-ke Oshi-no-ie Restored Pilgrim's Inn

At the height of Mt Fuji worship during the Edo period (1603–1868), Fuji-Yoshida was full of pilgrims' inns like this one, which has since been turned into a small museum.

Fujisan World Heritage Center

Learn more about Mt Fuji's spiritual and geological history via interactive displays at this (free) visitors centre. Near Kawaguchi-ko.

Fuji Sengen-jinja

Proper pilgrimages up Mt Fuji begin with a visit to historic Fuji Sengen-jinja in Fuji-Yoshida.

♨ Onsen

Benifuji-no-yu

Hot-spring complex with indoor and outdoor baths and grand Fuji vistas. Lots of bathing options, and saunas, too. Near Yamanaka-ko. No tattoos.

Fuji Chobo-no-yu Yurari

Indoor and outdoor baths, including ones that can be rented privately (for an extra fee). Mt Fuji views from some. On the main road, south of Sai-ko. No tattoos.

🎡 Amusement Parks & Ski Resorts

Fuji-Q Highland

One of Japan's best amusement parks, especially for roller coasters. It has its own train station, one stop west of Fujisan Station.

Fujiten Snow Resort

Small, family-friendly resort in the northern foothills of Mt Fuji, with Fuji views from the slopes. Sledging and play area for children.

Fujiten Snow Resort.

SMOLAW/SHUTTERSTOCK ©

⛺ Guesthouses & Campsites

Hitsuki Guesthouse ¥

Over 400 years old, this Fuji-Yoshida pilgrim lodge has been retooled into a guesthouse by its 18th-generation owner.

K's House Mt Fuji ¥

Simple but comfortable guesthouse in Kawaguchi-ko, great for meeting hikers and swapping info. Staff speak English.

Koan ¥

Chilled campsite on the edge of picturesque Motosu-ko. No reservations required, but check the homepage before setting out.

🍜 Hotpot, BBQ & Noodles

Sakurada Udon ¥

Sample local 'Yoshida udon' at this unassuming (but well-regarded) restaurant. On the main street in Fuji-Yoshida.

Tenka-chaya ¥¥

In the mountains above Kawaguchi-ko, overlooking the lake and Mt Fuji, this long-running restaurant serves *hoto* with local mushrooms.

Hoto Fudo ¥¥

This establishment has several branches, including one across from Kawaguchi-ko Station, and serves its *hoto* in a broth thickened with sweet potato and pumpkin.

Sanrokuen ¥¥

Grill skewers over traditional *irori* charcoal pits in an old thatched-roof building. Reservations recommended. In Kawaguchi-ko.

🛍 Sake, Souvenirs & Markets

Ide Sake Brewery

Reserve ahead for an English-language tour of this long-running Kawaguchi-ko brewery (21 generations!) that uses Fuji spring water.

Aokigahara Forest.

TSUICHI/SHUTTERSTOCK ©

FUJI FIVE LAKES REVIEWS

Michi-no-Eki Fuji-Yoshida

Road stop with a farmers market, local crafts and other souvenirs. Also excellent ice cream. Between Kawaguchi-ko and Yamanaka-ko.

🥾 Hiking Guides & Gear Rental

Fuji Mountain Guides

Professional and experienced bilingual guides lead both group and private tours up the Subashiri Trail, including transport from Tokyo and a night in a mountain hut. Gear rental available.

Fujiyama Guides

Hike Mt Fuji at your own pace, over two or three days, with a private, English-speaking, certified mountaineering guide, knowledgeable in local culture.

SORA no SHITA Kawaguchiko

Hiking-gear rentals, luggage storage, bicycle rentals, second-hand gear for sale and cool Fuji swag. Near Kawaguchi-ko Station.

Scan for more things to see, do and try in Fuji Five Lakes

CENTRAL
JAPAN ALPS

OUTDOORS | HIKING | HISTORY

**Experience
Central
Japan Alps
online**

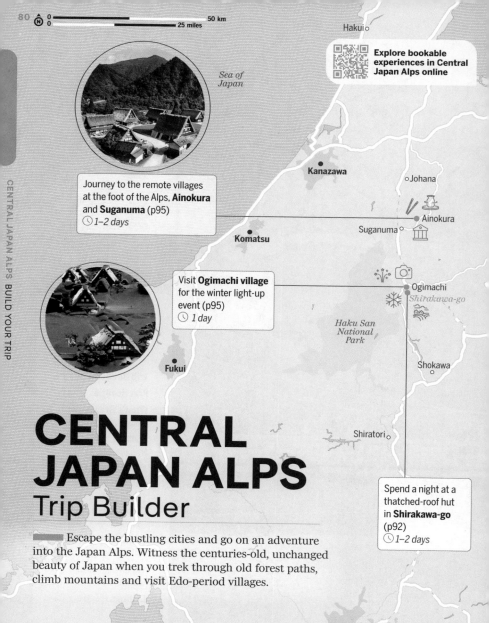

0
0

50 km

25 miles

Sea of Japan

Hakui

Explore bookable experiences in Central Japan Alps online

Journey to the remote villages at the foot of the Alps, **Ainokura** and **Suganuma** (p95)
🕐 *1–2 days*

Kanazawa

Johana

Ainokura

Suganuma

Komatsu

Visit **Ogimachi village** for the winter light-up event (p95)
🕐 *1 day*

Ogimachi

Shirakawa-go

Haku San National Park

Shokawa

Fukui

CENTRAL JAPAN ALPS
Trip Builder

Escape the bustling cities and go on an adventure into the Japan Alps. Witness the centuries-old, unchanged beauty of Japan when you trek through old forest paths, climb mountains and visit Edo-period villages.

Shiratori

Spend a night at a thatched-roof hut in **Shirakawa-go** (p92)
🕐 *1–2 days*

See autumn leaves and ravines from aboard the **Kurobe Gorge Railway** (p96)
🕐 *1 day*

Hike the Japan Alps, camp out in meadows and catch the sacred Hotaka Shrine Boat Festival at **Kamikochi** (88)
🕐 *2–4 days*

Taste some of Japan's best sake at Takayama's **Sanmachi-suji district** (p84)
🕐 *½ day*

Walk the path of old-time travellers via the **Nakasendo Ttrail** (p86)
🕐 *1 day*

Escape the modern world to the Edo-period post towns of **Magome** and **Tsumago** (p86)
🕐 *1 day*

Toyama-wan

Uozu

oyama

Tateyama

Kuronagi Onsen

Hakuba

Obuse

Nagano

Shinano-omachi

Chubu-Sangaku National Park

Ueda

Azumino

Kamikochi

Matsumoto

Hida

Takayama

Shiojiri

Suwa

Narai

Yabuhara

Nagiso

Tsumago

Magome

Iida

Nakatsugawa

CAGE/SHUTTERSTOCK ©, BEIBAOKE/SHUTTERSTOCK ©, TUPUNGATO/SHUTTERSTOCK ©, MILOSZ MASLANKA/SHUTTERSTOCK ©

Practicalities

WIRE DOG/SHUTTERSTOCK ©

ARRIVING

Central Japan International Airport Get to central Nagoya by bus (¥1200, 80 minutes) or train (¥1230, 30 minutes). Buy tickets upon arrival; no reservation required. The bus arrives at Meitetsu Bus Terminal – ideal for transferring to a highway bus. The train goes to Meitetsu Nagoya Station, for easy transfer to JR trains.

JR Nagoya Station Reach destinations around the Japan Alps from here by transferring to express trains and shinkansen (bullet trains).

HOW MUCH FOR A

Set meal
¥1500

Coffee at a cafe
¥500

Bottle of sake
¥2000

GETTING AROUND

Train A quicker way to travel across prefectures. Timetables are easily accessed online and a spot is usually guaranteed. However, trains may be less frequent in more rural areas and some walking is required.

Highway bus Buses can often take you straight to your destination. Shirakawa-go and Kamikochi are best accessed by bus. Some buses can't be reserved, so arrive early to get a spot.

Walking A fair bit of walking is required between stations, bus stops and your destination. All public transport will leave right on the dot, so allow plenty of time to head back.

WHEN TO GO

MAR–MAY
National parks reopen in April; cherry-blossom season is from late March

JUN–AUG
Cool and temperate, ideal for outdoor activities; some crowds in late summer

SEP–NOV
Fine weather with cool breeze; see autumn leaves from late October

DEC–FEB
Heavy snowfall from late December; busiest season at Shirakawa-go

TOP: SITTHICHOK CHAIPROM/SHUTTERSTOCK ©

EATING & DRINKING

Takayama The food haven of the Alps, where you can have beautifully marbled Hida beef, followed by exquisite locally brewed sake. Save space in your stomach, because with the variety of delicious street food here, you'll be eating all day.

Yaki-zakana A common dish found across the region is *yaki-zakana* (grilled fish). You'll find it served whole, head and all, and sometimes skewered on a stick. Many traditional restaurants circle the skewered fish around an *irori* (hearth), giving it a woody, charred flavour.

Must-try street food	Best soba noodles
Hida Kotte-ushi (p98)	Keiseian (p98)

CONNECT & FIND YOUR WAY

Wi-fi Get free wi-fi at stations, visitors centres and most tourist sites. To stay connected, rent a pocket wi-fi or buy a prepaid SIM card from the airport or online at Japan Wireless.

Navigation Use Google Maps for detailed public transport schedules and walking routes. Large maps are common around town if you need to get centred.

WHERE TO STAY

You may be checking in and out of hotels on your trip through the Alps – stay at accessible towns to keep that to a minimum.

Place	Pro/Con
Nagoya	Major transport hub, with a range of hotels and guesthouses to suit any budget.
Takayama	Accessible from Nagoya; good base for taking the bus to Shirakawa-go and Gokayama.
Kamikochi	A selection of camping grounds, lodges and hotels are located within the national park.
Shirakawa-go	*Gassho-zukuri* (thatched-roof huts) for a special stay in the quiet countryside.
Magome or Tsumago	Rest and relax here if walking the Nakasendo trail.

REGIONAL TRAVEL PASS

Get unlimited rides on JR trains using the Alpine-Takayama-Matsumoto Area Tourist Pass (¥18,850; touristpass.jp). It's valid for five days and available through travel agents or major JR stations.

MONEY

Shops in rural areas seldom accept cards, although some might. Carry at least ¥10,000 in cash at all times. Head to the visitors centre in any area to look for tourist discount tickets and transport passes.

10 What's Brewing in
TAKAYAMA

SAKE | FOOD | CRAFTS

What makes good sake? Japan's Holy Land of Sake has the definitive answer and invites you to come find out. Sake brewing has taken place in Takayama for hundreds of years, but a stroll through the town is also a feast for the senses. From fragrant rice wine to delicate wood grains, here's what to taste, see, touch and discover.

KAPI NG/SHUTTERSTOCK ©

🗺 How to

Getting here Takayama is easily accessible from the Kansai area (Nagoya, Kyoto, Osaka) on the JR Hida Limited Express. If travelling from Tokyo, a JR Pass (¥33,610) is recommended.

When to go Sake lovers should visit in March when the Nombe Festival takes place for the ultimate sake-brewery-hopping and tasting experience.

Sanmachi-suji district Most breweries, shops and historical buildings dating from the Edo period are located here.

ITHITMHA/SHUTTERSTOCK ©

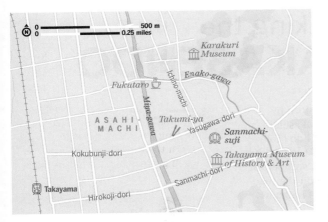

Takayama map showing Karakuri Museum, Fukutaro, Ichino-machi, Enako-gawa, Miya-gawa, ASAHI-MACHI, Takumi-ya, Yasugawa-dori, Sanmachi-suji, Sanmachi-dori, Takayama Museum of History & Art, Kokubunji-dori, Takayama, Hirokoji-dori. Scale: 500 m / 0.25 miles.

Above left Lacquerware shop.
Below left Goheimochi.

Feast Your Senses in the Old Town

Fine (rice) wine Clear water collected from the northern Japan Alps and locally harvested rice go into every batch of the exceptional sake brewed in Takayama. There are six individual breweries within the town, each offering tasting sessions for their signature sake. To spot a brewery, look out for a large cedar ball hanging out the front, called *sugidama*.

Street food The aroma of charcoal fires and food on the grill waft through Takayama, a place that is every street-food lover's dream. Must-try items are Hida beef skewers and *goheimochi* (rice cake slathered in sweet miso served on a popsicle stick). Look out for some other treats too: juicy Hida beef bun, crispy beef croquette, and adorable cat-faced *manju* (bun filled with sweet-bean paste).

Woodcarvings and lacquerware Lacquerware unique to Takayama is known as *Hida shunkei* – dinnerware coated in a clear lacquer that draws out the natural beauty of the wood underneath. Wooden ornaments can be found in shops around the city too, hand-carved by artisans out of yew using only chisels in a method called *ichii ittobori*.

Clockwork puppets Takayama's **Karakuri Museum** is a testament to the town's artisanship. Each *karakuri ningyo* puppet housed here is constructed out of clockwork, and depicts some well-known figures from Japanese history and mythology. See them in action at the museum, or catch them on a float during the town's spring and autumn festivals.

Sugidama

Seeing a large sphere hanging above the entrance to a building is how you identify a sake brewery, but the *sugidama* is significant in one other way.

Fashioned out of fresh cedar sprigs, the *sugidama* starts out bright green when it's first put in place. The eye-catching ornament is a brewery's way of signalling to passers-by that the year's brewing is complete and that it's time to enjoy fresh sake.

When it's put up, the *sugidama* is left for a year, slowly turning brown until it's replaced the same time next year.

11 Walking the
NAKASENDO

HISTORY | WALKING | NATURE

Travel like a feudal lord by walking sections of the Nakasendo, a trail that once connected Edo (Tokyo) to Kyoto. Though parts of the trail have been lost to development, snippets of the past can still be seen on the road between the post towns of Magome and Tsumago.

How to

Getting here Easiest access to the Kiso Valley is from Nagoya on the JR Chuo line. From Nakatsugawa Station, it's a 30-minute bus ride to Magome.

When to go Any season. Walking the trail in winter may require extra gear.

Easy trekking Head from Magome towards Tsumago for a mostly downhill walk. There is a hand-carry luggage-forwarding service at ¥1000 per piece.

A memento Buy a special card (¥300) at Magome's visitors centre and get it stamped in Tsumago for a certificate of your journey.

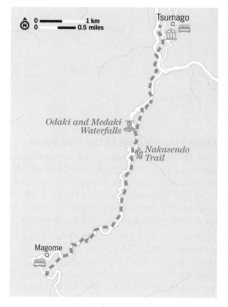

In the Footsteps of Shoguns

Edo revisited Strolling around the towns of **Magome** and **Tsumago** feels like travelling back in time. Well-preserved buildings from centuries past flank the streets; within are shops, inns and teahouses to spend an afternoon, soaking in the old-town atmosphere.

Forest path The Nakasendo trail is 530km long, but the section connecting Magome and Tsumago is a beginner-friendly 9km stretch. You can experience a little of what journeying during the Edo period might have been like. Walk on cobblestone paths through serene forests dotted with ancient monuments, and past the gushing **Odaki** and **Medaki** waterfalls to arrive at Tsumago after a rewarding three-hour journey.

Historical lodgings In the past, post towns were important as rest stops for travellers and inns

Above right Sign on the Nakasendo.
Below right Certificate of completion from Tsumago.

🏔 What are Post Towns?

Post towns, or *shukuba*, played a crucial role during the Edo period, when travel across the country was on horseback.

Existing along the Five Routes of Edo, these towns were designated by the shogunate as bases that would provide travellers with a place to rest. Just as importantly, they were responsible for forwarding goods and letters from the government to their intended recipients.

Because *shukuba* means 'a place of lodging', the name of each town is followed by the suffix *-juku* (eg Magome-juku), so that travellers can be sure that lodging is up ahead.

were significant landmarks. Tsumago has a reconstructed *honjin*, an inn for higher status guests, and a well-preserved *waki-honjin*, a separate building for common travellers, which now serves as a museum.

Stay the night Some of the old buildings lining the post towns have been converted into inns and guesthouses with modern facilities, while maintaining the buildings' traditional look. There are about a dozen in Magome and Tsumago, with some available to book online (japaneseguesthouses.com).

12 Adventures at KAMIKOCHI

ALPINE VIEWS | NATURE | HIKING

The term 'Japan Alps' was coined right here at Kamikochi, where snowy mountain vistas, reflective ponds and green meadows converge into an otherworldly paradise. Pack your outdoor gear and hiking boots – it's time to climb mountains, splash in the rivers, and camp out under the stars right in the heart of the Japan Alps.

How to

Getting here Catch a direct bus from Nagano Station (2½ hours). A bus trip from Takayama is also possible, stopping first at Hirayu Onsen (1½ hours).

When to go During the cool, verdant summer; the park is open April to November.

Bundle up Temperatures can dip below 10° C, even in summer. Pack a warm jacket and rain gear.

Where to stay Set up camp at designated areas, or book a nearby lodge or hotel.

Tokusawa-en (5km); Chogatake (9km)

Kamikochi Visitor Centre

Kamikochi Tourist Information Center

Kappa-bashi

Kamikochi Bus Station

Taisho-ike

Chubu-Sangaku National Park

Yake-dake (12km)

Mirror ponds, alpine views
Kamikochi's nature takes your breath away. The sky and the mountains are reflected in perfect symmetry at **Taisho-ike**, formed with the eruption of Yake-dake. Take your time walking across **Kappa-bashi**, an iconic bridge on the sparkling Azusa-gawa near the bus terminal – spectacular alpine views unfold on either side.

Hiking the Japan Alps
Beginner and expert hikers alike can attempt the many trekking routes in this vast national park. Those inexperienced can make a leisurely trek to **Tokusawa** to see an alpine meadow and a

Above right Hiker, Japan Alps.
Below right Taisho-ike.

BLUE PLANET STUDIO/SHUTTERSTOCK ©

🚶 Expert Tips

Those looking for a more rigorous hike can try the journey up to the **Karasawa Col**. Come in early spring with crampons!

    Adventurous travellers can try the **Yariga-take ascent**, followed by a hair-raising traverse of the **Daikiretto ridge**. Technical climbers will also enjoy rock climbing at the **Byobu Iwa rock face**.

Tips by William Habington
freelance writer, translator and expert on Kamikochi.
@nokori3byo

side of rocky Mae-hotaka-dake. Seasoned hikers can try climbing **Chogatake** or **Yake-dake**, among other peaks. More advanced trails require an overnight stay in a tent or cabin, plus filling out a trekking itinerary (go-nagano.net/climbing).

Festivals The most notable events are the **Kaizansai** (mountain opening) ceremony in April, when the park first opens to visitors, and the **Myojin-ike Ofune Matsuri** (Hotaka Shrine Boat Festival) in October, when ceremony boats sail across the pond of Myojin-ike. Both are Shinto ceremonies, performed to pray for safe passage through the mountains and to give thanks.

PJJARUWAN/SHUTTERSTOCK ©

The Mythical Creatures of Japan

DIVE INTO THE MYSTERIOUS WORLD OF YOKAI

At the centre of Kamikochi is a stately wooden bridge, Kappa-bashi. When it was built is unclear, but it was immortalised in the 1927 novel, *Kappa,* by Ryunosuke Akutagawa. A creature that dwells in the watery depths, the *kappa* is but one of Japan's spirits of the unknown.

Left *Tanuki.*
Centre Illustration of *Yotsuya kaidan,* a 19th-century ghost story.
Right *Kappa.*

The World of Yokai

Ghostly apparitions, inexplicable phenomena, animals that maybe aren't what they seem – these are what Japan calls *yokai*. Every culture has its own ghosts and spirits, but it isn't an exaggeration to say that Japan seemingly has a *yokai* version of everything, from completely made-up monsters to everyday objects and furry critters.

Haunted Objects

The popularity of *kaidan*, or the telling of ghost stories, was believed to have emerged during the Edo period. It was represented in written stories, drawings and *ukiyo-e* (woodblock prints). Stories of possessed daily objects were commonplace – a lantern that looks a little ghostly? It might be a *chochin-obake*, with eyes, an open mouth and a lolling tongue. Umbrellas can be *yokai* too; a popular character through the ages is the *kasa-obake*, a cyclops umbrella with two arms and a leg. Unlike some monsters that still carry an air of mystery, very little suggests that people believed these apparitions to be real, and they were possibly not even meant to frighten but merely entertain.

Animal Spirits

Even animals are not exempt from gaining *yokai* status. A popular animal that is sometimes considered a *yokai* is the Japanese racoon-dog, *tanuki*. It's a shape-shifting creature known for mischief, and there are tales of *tanuki* changing into tea kettles, humans and even Buddhist monks. Prominent folk tales like 'Kachi-kachi Yama' and 'Bunbuku Chagama' feature a *tanuki* playing pranks on people or generally being up to no good.

ARTOKOLORO/ALAMY STOCK PHOTO ©

AKSARA.K/SHUTTERSTOCK ©

Ghostly Apparitions

No ghost story is complete without haunting apparitions, and popular Japanese stories both modern and old are full of these. A woman with long flowing hair in a white kimono drifting alone on a cold winter night is *yuki-onna* (snow woman), ready to lure men into their cold graves. Horror-movie favourite Sadako from *The Ring* can also trace her origins back to a kind of Japanese ghost called *onryo*, a vengeful spirit crawling back from the afterlife to exact revenge.

> Japan seemingly has a *yokai* version of everything, from completely made-up monsters to everyday objects and furry critters.

Fictitious Monsters

The *kappa* is perhaps the most popular example of a *yokai*, appearing as sometimes cute and mostly harmless characters in anime and video games, as well as being Kappa-bashi's namesake. Often described as a slimy water creature with a beak, a shell on its back, and a dish on its head (plus a penchant for cucumbers), the *kappa* might not sound very frightening – until you hear of the sordid affairs it gets up to. It's said to have sucked the soul out of humans, drowned adults and children, and even consumed their flesh. So how was a bridge in picturesque Kamikochi named after this creature? Legends say that a *kappa* used to dwell in the waters under the bridge, though whether that's true remains a mystery.

📖 Yokai in Media

Yokai can be found everywhere in books and media. The manga *GeGeGe no Kitaro* by Shigeru Mizuki is a beloved series that brought *yokai* to modern audiences. More recently, the video game and anime series *Yo-kai Watch* has gained a popular following among schoolchildren.

For a taste of traditional Japanese ghost stories in English, the books *Kwaidan* and *In Ghostly Japan* by scholar of Japanese culture Lafcadio Hearn are the best places to start. Prime examples of *yokai* can also be seen in animated films from Studio Ghibli, including the shape-shifting old lady Yubaba from *Spirited Away,* and the ghostly little Kodama from *Princess Mononoke.*

13 Snowy Villages of
SHIRAKAWA-GO

WINTER | ARCHITECTURE | FARMSTAY

Nestled in a valley in the mountainous areas of Shirakawa-go and Gokayama are thousand-year-old villages with picture-perfect winter views and rustic architecture. Stay under the sloping roofs of the *gassho-zukuri* (thatch-roof huts) and get a taste of the quiet life in this remote region.

🏯 How to

Getting here/around
Shirakawa-go is accessible by bus from Nagoya, Takayama, Toyama and Kanazawa. Buses also go from Shirakawa-go to Gokayama.

When to go Visit in winter (December to February), for spectacular views of the village covered in snow; or in summer (June to August), when the climate is cool and comfortable.

Coffee and crafts
Shop for local crafts and warm up with a coffee at Shinkado in Ogimachi village. Look out for the sign out front that reads 心花洞.

Spending a Night at the Village

Several accommodation options are available at Shirakawa-go. Many choose to stay at a ryokan (inn), hotel or guesthouse, but there's one other option that can make your trip special – the farmstay.

Live like a local Small, family-run accommodation like some of the *gassho-zukuri* in the area are known as *minshuku*, which roughly translates to 'people lodging'. They are the Japanese version of quaint B&Bs – only in Shirakawa-go, you will be spending the night in a centuries-old farmhouse.

What it's like Spend the day exploring the village, then check in and warm up by the flaming *irori* (hearth) while your host prepares a dinner with ingredients fresh from the river and farms nearby. You may

🏠 Gassho-zukuri

The sloping thatched roofs of the village huts are the only ones found in Japan. The huts derived their name from the word *gassho*, which in Japanese means 'prayer hands', implying that the buildings resemble two hands pressed together in prayer.

Above left Village in Shirakawa-go.
Above right *Gassho-zukuri*, Gokayama.
Left *Irori* in a *minshuku*.

share the farmhouse with other guests and the host's family – it's a chance to make conversation and build connections over dinner around the hearth. At night, curl up in a futon laid out on tatami mats. Wake up to the sound of birds and splendid mountain views.

Amenities All *gassho-zukuri* houses retain their traditional, rustic interior, but most are fitted out with modern Western-style toilets and good bathing facilities.

Booking a stay All guests are limited to a night's stay at each farmhouse, and all payments must be made in cash (japaneseguesthouses.com).

World Heritage Villages

Three villages around the border between Gifu and Toyama prefectures make up one of Japan's most prominent Unesco World Heritage Sites. The most famous is Ogimachi village, located in Shirakawa-go district, while

𝒱 Local Cuisine

River-fish shioyaki Freshly caught fish from the nearby Sho-gawa, skewered whole, generously salted, and grilled around a traditional *irori* (hearth).

Goheimochi Rice dumplings slathered in a locally produced, sweet-tasting miso paste, skewered and grilled over charcoal. Sweet, salty and fragrant, all at the same time!

Hoba-miso Meat and vegetables covered in sweet miso paste, set atop a dried magnolia leaf and placed over a small charcoal burner to cook. A must-try.

Hida beef Beautifully marbled, melt-in-your-mouth beef from prized cattle raised within the region. Try it grilled, as sukiyaki hotpot, or with *hoba-miso*.

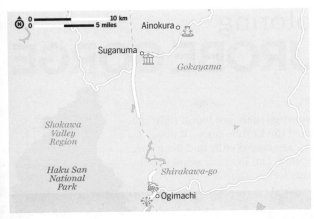

Left *Hoba-miso.*
Below *Washi* being made, Gokayama.

the villages of Ainokura and Suganuma belong to the Gokayama area.

Ogimachi This village has the largest number of *gassho-zukuri* huts, and is also the most visited. As people usually go in winter, it can be great to visit in summer and autumn when the village is quieter. A winter light-up event takes place on select weekends in January and February. Demand is high and reservations are required. Spending a night at a farmhouse in Ogimachi village guarantees you a spot.

Ainokura Watch the art of making traditional Gokayama *washi* (handmade paper) in this less populated *gassho-zukuri* village. Then have a go at making it yourself.

Suganuma This quiet village has nine *gassho-zukuri* houses. The **Gokayama Minzoku-kan** folklore museum has exhibits showcasing daily life in the village, and the Nitre Museum houses tools used for nitre production, a former major industry in Gokayama.

LEFT: TAWIN MUKDHARAKOSA/SHUTTERSTOCK ©.
RIGHT: ILENE PERLMAN/ALAMY STOCK PHOTO ©

Exploring
KUROBE GORGE

NATURE | RAIL | OUTDOORS

Some of Japan's best experiences are found right here in Kurobe Gorge. Hop aboard the Kurobe Gorge Railway for a spectacular scenic journey – see jagged cliffs and deep gorges bursting with colour in autumn, and hear the echoes as the railway rumbles through the deep tunnels.

PHUBET JUNTARUNGSEE/SHUTTERSTOCK ©

📷 Snapshot

The magnifcent Kurobe Gorge makes for picture-perfect shots anywhere along the railway. However, to snap a photo of the train rolling across the iconic bridge of Shin-Yamabiko-bashi, photographers and rail fans can wait at the **Yamabiko Observation Platform** outside Unazuki Station for the perfect moment.

🗺 Trip Notes

Getting here/around Travel to Kurobe Unazuki Onsen Station in Toyama Prefecture by bullet train. The railway journey starts here and ends at Keyaki-daira.

When to go The railway operates from mid-April to November. The best time to see the autumn foliage is from mid-October.

Choose your ride The standard windowless carriage is popular among shutterbugs. The windowed 1st- and 2nd-class carriages offer more comfort and protection from the elements for a small extra charge (kurotetu.co.jp).

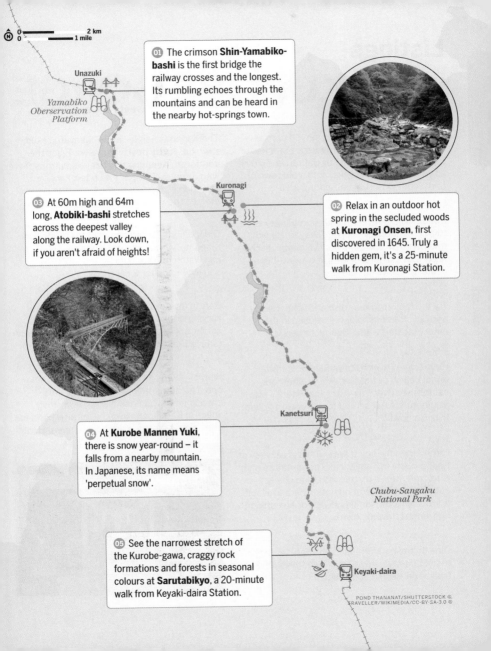

0 2 km
0 1 mile

Unazuki

Yamabiko Oberservation Platform

01 The crimson **Shin-Yamabiko-bashi** is the first bridge the railway crosses and the longest. Its rumbling echoes through the mountains and can be heard in the nearby hot-springs town.

Kuronagi

03 At 60m high and 64m long, **Atobiki-bashi** stretches across the deepest valley along the railway. Look down, if you aren't afraid of heights!

02 Relax in an outdoor hot spring in the secluded woods at **Kuronagi Onsen**, first discovered in 1645. Truly a hidden gem, it's a 25-minute walk from Kuronagi Station.

Kanetsuri

04 At **Kurobe Mannen Yuki**, there is snow year-round – it falls from a nearby mountain. In Japanese, its name means 'perpetual snow'.

Chubu-Sangaku National Park

05 See the narrowest stretch of the Kurobe-gawa, craggy rock formations and forests in seasonal colours at **Sarutabikyo**, a 20-minute walk from Keyaki-daira Station.

Keyaki-daira

POND THANANAT/SHUTTERSTOCK ©
TRAVELLER/WIKIMEDIA/CC-BY-SA-3.0 ©

Listings

BEST OF THE REST

 Local Flavours

Hida Kotte-ushi ¥

Juicy and fatty Hida beef is served here as *nigiri-zushi* atop a homemade rice cracker, topped with chives and special sauce. Enjoy it as you stroll around Takayama's old town or find a spot in the casual seating area.

Tōhoen ¥

Buy some cat-faced *manju* (dumplings) at this confectionery shop in Takayama's old town. A small box contains five *manju*, each filled with a different flavoured sweet-bean paste. Great for gifts!

Irori ¥¥

Try the famous *hoba-miso* and other hearty and delicious *teishoku* (set meals) in this eatery located within Ogimachi village.

Kamonji-goya ¥

Have *iwana* (river trout) grilled on a tradi-tional hearth at this Kamikochi landmark, established over 140 years ago. There's also a signature sake, served together with grilled fish in a bowl.

Gosenjaku Kitchen ¥¥

Family-friendly dining area with a great view of Kappa-bashi in Kamikochi. The signature dish is *sanzokuyaki*, a platter with fried chicken cutlet, but diverse menu options are available. It's inside Hotel Kamikochi; go for an early or late lunch to avoid crowds.

Keiseian ¥

Dine on fresh handmade soba noodles in this rustic Edo-style building in Magome with a traditional hearth at its centre.

Coffee, Sweets & Cosy Spaces

Cafe Ao ¥

This Japanese-style cafe in Takayama's old town has lovely courtyard views. Enjoy the comfortable seating and a relaxed atmosphere with a cup of coffee or green tea. Excellent selection of Japanese sweets; try the creamy *matcha* (powedered green tea) roll cake.

Yomongiya ¥

Old lodgings turned quaint cafe in historical Magome, with outdoor seating so you can watch the world go by. It doubles as a souvenir shop for local crafts.

Chabo Ebiya ¥

Cafe in an old-style building in Tsumago serving drinks and an array of Japanese confectionery. Drop by in summer for *kakigori* (shaved ice flavoured with syrup).

Cafe Grindelwald ¥¥

Warm lighting, a classic European aesthetic, and a giant mantelpiece complete with crackling firewood make this the cosiest space in Kamikochi. Stop by for afternoon tea and cake; it's inside Kamikochi Imperial Hotel.

Hida Folk Village.

MICHAEL GORDON/SHUTTERSTOCK ©

🏠 Traditional Stays

Shiroyama-kan ¥¥¥

This ryokan in Ogimachi village, built in the Meiji period, is now run entirely by one family. The ryokan only houses four groups of guests at a time, so advance booking is recommended.

Jyuemon ¥¥

A 300-year-old *gassho-zukuri* house providing farmstays in a quiet area at the very end of Ogimachi. Spend an evening by the hearth with other guests and enjoy a *shamisen* (three-stringed instrument) performance.

Fujioto ¥¥

Edo-period ryokan in Tsumago with cypress baths and rooms that overlook a gorgeous Japanese garden.

🏃 Outdoor Thrills

Kurobe Gorge Canyoning

Slip, slide, glide and dive into the blue waters at Kurobe Gorge with half-day canyoning tours, available April to November at Unazuki Onsen. Pack a swimsuit!

Satoyama Experience

See rivers, *sakura* (cherry blossoms) and rice fields against the mountains of Gifu Prefecture with Satoyama Experience. Join a guided cycling tour in the warmer months, or trek through thick layers of snow in winter. Tours depart from Hida-Furukawa near Takayama.

🏘 Historical Vibes

Hida Folk Village

Traditional houses from across the Hida region can all be seen in one place at this open-air museum in Takayama. Try your hand at local crafts by joining some of the workshops; no reservation required.

MOREGALLERY/SHUTTERSTOCK ©

Takayama Showa-kan.

Takayama Showa-kan

Slip back in time to Japan's Showa period at a Takayama museum. It's laid out like a small town, with recreated shops, restaurants and even a classroom.

Nagiso Town Museum

This museum in Tsumago is made up of three sections: two historical inns (*honjin* and *waki-honjin*) and a history museum. The *waki-honjin* – built using cypress wood, which was once banned from harvest – is especially popular.

Magome Waki-honjin Museum

A former secondary inn, meant for lower ranking travellers, now displays items that tell of Magome's history as a post town.

Tajima House Museum of Silk Culture

The only building in Ogimachi village of Shirakawa-go with exhibits pertaining to sericulture – the cultivation of silk worms. An informative look at what the *gassho-zukuri* houses were actually used for.

 Scan for more things to see, do and try in Central Japan Alps

KYOTO & NARA

HISTORY | CULTURE | ARCHITECTURE

Experience Kyoto & Nara online

TAKASHI IMAGES/SHUTTERSTOCK ©

Take time to wander around **Kinkaku-ji** and Kyoto's other famous sites (p116)
🕒 *1–2 days*

Osawa-no-ike

UKYO-KU

Kita Tenm gu

Hop on a bicycle and spend a day touring the cherry blossoms. **Hirano Shrine** is very popular (p112)
🕒 *1 day*

SAGA

Kameyama-koen

Iwatayama Monkey Park

NISHIKYO-KU

KYOTO & NARA
Trip Builder

Kyoto's old traditions epitomise delicacy and gentility, as expressed in a grand *kaiseki* dinner, a quiet temple garden, or an evening with a geisha. The Grand Buddha of Nara is perfectly framed by the natural surroundings of the ancient capital.

Teujin-gawa

Katsura-gawa

MINAMI-K

Explore bookable experiences in Kyoto and Nara online

PURIPAT LERTPUNYAROJ/SHUTTERSTOCK ©, ANDRIY BLOKHIN/ SHUTTERSTOCK ©, NISHIHAMA/SHUTTERSTOCK ©, LEONID ANDRONOV/SHUTTERSTOCK ©, TOOYKRUB/SHUTTERSTOCK ©

MUKO-SHI

KITA-KU

Kyoto Botanical Gardens

Plan your stay around Kyoto's **food culture**: elaborate *kaiseki*, rustic *obanzai-ryori* and simple *shojin-ryori* meals (p110)

🕐 *2–3 hours*

naokayama-en

Takano-gawa

Tadasu-no-mori

KAMIGYO-KU

SAKYO-KU

Kyoto Imperial Palace Park

Shira-kawa

Ponder the seasons on the **Path of Philosophy** (p112)

🕐 *½–1 day*

Okazaki-koen

Sanjo Bridge

Nara Inset

NAKAGYO-KU

Pontocho

GION

Find serenity in the face of the world's largest bronze **Buddha** (p122)

🕐 *¼ day*

Nara-koen

Giro Giro Hitoshina

Kamo-gawa

See the world in a bowl of **tea**, in its birthplace (p106)

🕐 *1–2 hours*

Shosei-en

SHIMOGYO-KU

Pass the afternoon strolling the historic lushness of **Nara-koen** (p124)

🕐 *½–1 day*

Fushimi Inari-Taisha

Walk the ancient **Yamanobe-no-michi** trail to the birthplace of Japanese sake (p126)

🕐 *½–1 day*

FUSHIMI-KU

Nara (40km; see Inset)

0 — 5 km
0 — 2.5 miles

0 — 2 km
0 — 1 miles

Practicalities

LEXOSN/SHUTTERSTOCK ©

ARRIVING

Trains Depart Kansai Airport twice an hour for the 75-minute trip to Kyoto, costing about ¥3500. Tickets can be purchased adjacent to the boarding gates (no reservations required). Shinkansen (bullet trains) from Tokyo Station make the trip for ¥14,000 in just over two hours. From Osaka, express trains depart frequently for the 30-minute, ¥500 trip. Take the Keihan or JR lines from Kyoto Station to Nara. The journey takes 45 minutes and costs around ¥700.

HOW MUCH FOR A

Matcha ice cream
¥350

Bento box
¥900–1200

Temple visit
¥500

GETTING AROUND

Suica and Pasmo Rechargeable, prepaid Suica and Pasmo cards work on all Kyoto trains, subways and buses. Purchase from any touchscreen ticket-vending machine. Both require a ¥500 deposit, which is refunded (along with any remaining charge) when you return the pass to any ticket window.

Bicycle Kyoto's limited train service, crowded buses and flat terrain make the city ideal for cycling. Bicycles can be rented from numerous locations throughout the city for ¥1000 per day. Many hotels offer free bicycles to guests.

Taxi Taxis are numerous in Kyoto. Most drivers don't speak English, but as GPS location can be entered by telephone number, have this on hand for those difficult-to-find destinations.

WHEN TO GO

DEC–FEB
Winters in Kyoto are notoriously cold; pack accordingly

MAR–MAY
The warming days bring an array of flowers; probably Kyoto's best season

JUN–SEP
Kyoto is one of the hottest places in Japan; hot and very sticky

OCT–NOV
A very pleasant time to visit, but occasional typhoons

TOP: OLIVER STREWE/GETTY IMAGES ©

EATING & DRINKING

Sanjo Bridge Hundreds of restaurants can be found on the main boulevards and side streets to the west of Sanjo Bridge. Let the menus and plastic food on display be your guide.

Pontocho This narrow alley is lined with little eateries that offer views over the river. If visiting in summer, be sure to take a meal on the wooden *yuka* decks built above a cooling stream. One of the best is Karyu, offering affordable *kaiseki* in a restored teahouse.

Must-try	Best matcha soft cream
Tofu doughnuts at Nishiki Market (p128)	Just about everywhere

CONNECT & FIND YOUR WAY

Wi-fi The free KYOTO_WiFi can be found at over 600 hotspots throughout the city. However, users must send an email in order to get an access code, so be sure to register before coming to town.

Navigation Built on a grid, Kyoto is one of the easier cities to navigate.

BEAT THE CROWDS

Most temples and many shrines open early, so visit before the crowds. Sites tend to be clustered, so divide the city into grids and walk.

WHERE TO STAY

One of the world's top travel destinations, Kyoto has no shortage of accommodation for every budget. Split your stay between a quaint Airbnb and one of the city's classic hotels.

Neighbourhood	Pro/Con
Gion	Traditional geisha quarter. Somewhat crowded, but with plenty of restaurants and quiet streets after dark.
Karasuma	Home to numerous hotels, close to bustling nightlife and along the convenient Karasuma subway line.
Kyoto Station area	Convenient for those making day trips to Osaka, Kobe or Nara. No shortage of restaurants and shopping nearby, but a bit busy.
Arashiyama	This popular area on Kyoto's western edge empties out after dark. An early-morning walk in the bamboo forest promises photos free of crowds.
Higashiyama	For a longer stay, rent an Airbnb in semi-rural Higashiyama and live like a local.

MONEY

Cash is king in Japan, and often the only option, though cards are beginning to be more widely used. Have lunch at local neighbourhood shops, before splurging at dinner.

15 Taking a Tea CEREMONY

ART | CULTURE | DRINK

As much of Kyoto culture developed around tea, teahouses can be found throughout the city, and taking tea is a must for visitors. Enjoy the host's hospitality, as powdered green tea is whisked into a froth with incredible speed, accompanied by sweets to balance the flavour. The experience offers a refreshing break from the outside world.

🖾 How to

Arranging a tea experience While many Kyoto hotels can arrange a tea experience, a handful of places in town can be contacted directly for a more authentic experience, offered in English.

How much A typical one-hour ceremony costs around ¥2500, or ¥5000 if a kimono option is offered.

Top tip A highly caffeinated burst of green *matcha* in the late afternoon is a wonderful way to refresh you for the nightlife ahead.

At its most simple, a tea gathering entails drinking hot *matcha* tea after eating Japanese sweets. Yet the experience is highly refined: in the way a guest holds a bowl, or how the host prepares the boiling water and handles the utensils.

As the Japanese of the past had no access to museums, the tearoom became a repository of Japanese art itself, and even today, the flowers, incense and hanging scrolls are carefully chosen, often to reflect the season. At its most refined,

Above right Japanese sweets.
Below right Tea ceremony.

☕ Tea on the Go

Kyoto is filled with shops catering to tea culture. **Ippodo** is perhaps best known, with roots going back to 1717. Three-hundred-year-old **Marukyu Koyamaen** sells tea grown at its estate in Uji. **Yamashita** on Teranouchi-dori has been selling tea ceremony utensils that are works of art since 1850.

the process becomes meditative. Randy Channell Soei, owner of Ran Hotei, states: 'Both host and guest strive to grasp the essence of harmony, respect, and purity, allowing one to experience tranquillity, while sharing a bowl of tea.' Yet he feels that it should be enjoyable rather than formal: 'I hope that people will consider tea more than just a drink. Ideally it is sharing time with others and appreciating the moment.'

Maikoya Kyoto leads the kimono-clad guest to make their own cup of tea, with a variety of displays that explain tea culture. **En** offers an accessible, simpler affair held at various times throughout the day. **Ran Hotei** allows for a more relaxed, tailored experience in a full-on cafe that offers food, drink and original teas to take home.

With expert insights from Peter MacIntosh

Peter is a Kyoto-based, Canadian photographer, artist, entrepreneur and geisha culture guru.

petermacintosh.com, @kyotopmac

An Evening in the Floating World

DINING | DRINK | ENTERTAINMENT

Much like Kyoto itself, part of the appeal of the geisha is her cultivated mystique. It's possible to share an evening with these classical performers, though whether that entails dinner or simply drinks is based on the dimensions of your wallet.

Left *Geiko*, Gion.
Centre *Maiko*, Gion.
Right *Maiko* performing during *ozakashi*.

MORUMOTTO/SHUTTERSTOCK ©

Recognised as an integral symbol of Kyoto, geisha are referred to locally as *geiko*, with their younger apprentices being called *maiko*. Divided between the city's five geisha districts, known as *hanamachi* (flower towns), the current population stands at about 240.

The term *gei* means performance, and training begins after finishing junior high school. The initial five-year curriculum consists of dance, music, poetry and calligraphy, but studies continue throughout their career. For a young Japanese woman, it's the best way to get such a comprehensive understanding of her own culture.

Access to the floating world was once incredibly exclusive, permissible only with an introduction. Besides private parties at teahouses and restaurants, geisha could be hired for big social events. Because of recent economic difficulties, restrictions have loosened to keep the tradition alive.

So where can the visitor see geisha? A chance encounter with anyone in a city of 1.5 million is obviously difficult, but if you stroll any of the *hanamachi* in the early evening you'll have the best chance of catching a glimpse of a *geiko* or *maiko* as they head out to their first engagement. There has been a backlash against foreign tourists crowding the women, so be sure to give them space. You can tell a *maiko* from a *geiko* as the former wear colourful kimonos with longer sleeves and ornate hairpins. *Geiko* wear simpler kimonos with shorter sleeves, and fewer accessories in their hair.

The most affordable way to see a performance is to attend one of the five annual Dance Festivals, usually in spring and autumn. *Maiko* also perform daily at the Gion Corner.

PR IMAGE FACTORY/E/SHUTTERSTOCK ©

IRINA WILHAUK/SHUTTERSTOCK ©

An evening of geisha entertainment for two – over a private *ozashiki* dinner – starts at around ¥90,000, and includes one *maiko*, one *geiko* and a *shamisen* player. Peter MacIntosh admits that, 'People say geisha entertainment is expensive, and they are right. These women are highly trained professionals dedicated to the arts and they are expensive to hire. You get what you pay for.' Some inns offer a more affordable two-hour group dinner with a maiko for about ¥20,000 per person.

Most geisha *ozashiki* take place in a formal setting so it's important to dress smartly, but comfortably. 'To enjoy geisha entertainment as a foreign visitor, you must put aside any preconceived ideas you have from movies and books and let the women take you into their world where you, the customer – whether it be man, women or child – will get a glimpse into the floating world and traditional culture,' MacIntosh says.

A *kaiseki* meal is the first order of business, throughout which your entertainer will make small talk. Performances follow, usually songs and dances often seen in traditional Japanese theatre arts. But the most memorable part of the evening is certain to be the traditional party games involving wordplay and penalty drinking. MacIntosh says his 'customers always comment on how much fun the entertainment was and how they were surprised by how the *maiko/geiko* were so down to earth and not overly formal'.

> *Maiko* wear colourful kimonos with longer sleeves and ornate hairpins. *Geiko* wear simpler kimonos with shorter sleeves, and fewer accessories in their hair.

📖 Best Geisha Books

While Arthur Golden's novel *Memoirs of a Geisha* is the best known, *Geisha of Gion*, the autobiography of his research subject Mineko Iwasaki, is far more accurate. *Geisha* by American anthropologist Liza Dalby details her immersive experience performing in an unofficial capacity at an *ozashiki*. Lesley Downer's *Geisha: The Remarkable Truth Behind the Fiction* was written from the perspective of living in Miyagawa-cho, one of Kyoto's five geisha districts. *Madame Sadayakko*, also written by Downer, tells the story of Japan's most celebrated geisha, who entertained European statesmen and royalty of the early 20th century, before retiring to tour the world as a travelling actress.

16 Art at the End of Your **CHOPSTICKS**

FOOD | ART | CULTURE

When people think of Japanese food, they tend to think of *kaiseki*. And Kyoto is its capital. Besides a few planned 'big' meals, leave things to chance by popping into any place that looks inviting. If you get burned out, you can still remain a purist by trying foreign fare made with local ingredients. Miso pizza or *yuzu* burgers, anyone?

How to

Planning ahead Kyoto's food culture has become incredibly well known over the past decade, so if you have a place in mind, it is best to book as early as possible. Otherwise, ask around once you get to town.

Top tip Don't overdo it. It is easy to burn out by too many bombastic dinners, so give yourself a night or two off to find something simpler near your hotel.

Simplicity *Kaiseki*, the meal taken during a full tea ceremony, has evolved from humble roots into an art form. Consisting of a series of small courses arranged to delight the eye as well as the palate, a *kaiseki* meal builds slowly, consisting of an appetiser, a raw dish, a simmered dish, a grilled dish and a steamed course. With so many choices on offer, chefs love to get creative. The talented chef at **Mavo** seems destined for Michelin status, though you will pay well. Moderately priced **Giro Giro Hitoshina** has been fondly called 'punk

Above right Sashimi.
Below right *Shojin-ryori*.

LOTTE DAVIES/LONELY PLANET ©

KO FUJIMURA/GETTY IMAGES ©

🛍 Japanese Knives

With the end of the feudal period, samurai sword-makers shifted their knowledge to culinary knives. These high-quality Japanese knives deserve their reputation. Aritsugi in **Nishijin Market** is the best-known, patronised by local chefs. Smaller **Shinto** offers a more personal experience.

kaiseki', and a counter seat is essential for watching the young team create their art. The English-speaking chef at **Another C** can talk you through your meal, while **Hachiyoshi** is a small and affordable spot near the Path of Philosophy.

Home cooking Obanzai-ryori means cuisine native to Kyoto. It's made from in-season, locally sourced and affordable ingredients. **Menami** is the classic, while **Kikkoya** has been getting some attention for it's simple fare. **Omuraya** offers takeaway bento boxes to enjoy beside the Kamo-gawa (the river).

Buddhist fare Shojin-ryori refers to the meals eaten in temples, from an authentic lunch at **Izusen** within Daitoku-ji to Tenryuji's-Bib Michelin-ranked **Shigatsu**.

17 Pedalling the
PETALS

NATURE | FOOD | FESTIVAL

For a tree that doesn't bear fruit, *sakura* (cherry blossom) certainly has a large following. In the mind of many visitors, it is the definitive symbol of Japan. Flowering for a mere two weeks, with full bloom lasting just days, the fleeting pink petals are a lesson in impermanence in the Japanese mind, something the visitor who has mistimed their trip can well understand.

STUDIO.S/SHUTTERSTOCK ©

🗺 How to

When to go The *sakura* flower from very late March into early April, though dates vary year to year and are impossible to predict. Your best bet is to plan to be in country on April 1st, and you will most likely find the trees in some stage of bloom.

Where to go Rent a bicycle at EMUSICA Demachiyanagi, and follow the pink petals towards the Path of Philosophy.

LINA SHATALOVA/GETTY IMAGES ©

Map labels: Hirano Shrine; Takano-gawa; EMUSICA; Path of Philosophy (Tetsugaku-no-Michi); KAMIGYO-KU; Kyoto Imperial Palace Park; Kamo-gawa; SAKYO-KU; Okazaki Canal; NAKAGYO-KU; GION; Maruyama-koen; HIGASHIYAMA-KU; 0 — 2 km; 0 — 1 miles; N

Above left *Sakura*.
Below left Hirano Shrine.

Slow awakening The fleeting beauty of the *sakura* petals is the ideal manifestation of the impermanence of life, as they come and go within two weeks. The appearance of the flowers also means that winter is officially over, a welcome sight in a country devoid of interior heating. While the Yoshino *sakura* gets the most attention due to their omnipresence, the weeping *shidare-zakura* blooms like the slow-motion burst of pink fireworks. Purple *yamazakura* light up the mountainsides above, a colourful enticement to any hike.

Forest for the trees Even the briefest walk will bring you into contact with the unmistakable pink flowers, from the biggest temple grounds down to the smallest park. Throughout the country, you'll see people picnicking beneath the petals, with their boxed *bento* lunch and favourite beverage. The best way to find your own private spot in Kyoto is to rent a bicycle and ride the city. Follow waterways in particular, along the Path of Philosophy, then down the Keage Incline to the Okazaki Canal. The Kamo-gawa is a lovely and lively ride, and you can choose from literally hundreds of trees for one to call your own.

Trees for the forest After finding a quiet place for your own personal *hanami* (blossom viewing), seek out the more popular spots and join the party. Having the history, **Hirano Shrine** is one of the city's most famous, while **Maruyama-koen** will have a more relaxed feel.

🌿 Fleeting Pink

Sakura weren't always awarded the status they now hold. Traditionally, it was the late winter-blooming plum tree that was revered, a tradition originating in China.

The genteel nobility of the Heian period (794–1185) began to give the *sakura* pre-eminence and, by the Middle Ages, the tradition of viewing the cherry blossoms was firmly established within the warrior class. The five-day *hanami* party held by warlord Toyotomi Hideyoshi in 1594 was attended by 5000 guests.

With the coming of the modern age in the late 19th century, the custom spread across all classes.

A mass planting was undertaken after WWII to raise the spirits of the exhausted nation.

A Year in
FLOWERS

01 Plum blossoms
(late Feb–early Mar)
The first floral har-
binger of spring,
ume can be found
nationwide, but popular
spots include Kyoto's
Kitano Tenman-gu,
and Kyu Shiba Rikyu in
Tokyo.

02 Cherry blossoms
(late Mar–early Apr)
Japan's unofficial
national flower
can be widely seen
everywhere. One
favourite is along the
Meguro-gawa in Tokyo.

03 Wisteria
(late Apr–early May)
Often seen climbing
the trellises of many
parks. Try Tokyo's
Kameido Tenjin, or
Byodo-in in Kyoto.

04 Hydrangea
(mid-Jun–mid-Jul)
These multicoloured
gems line the paths of

Mimuroto-ji in Kyoto,
Hasedera in Kamakura,
and Yatadera Temple
in Nara.

05 Lotus
(mid-Jul–mid-Aug)
Buddhism's favourite
flower can be best seen
at Shinobazu-ike in
Tokyo, Hokongo-in in
Kyoto, or Mizunomori

Water Botanical Garden beside Biwa-ko.

06 Irises
(late May–Jul)
Favourite spots include Nezu Museum and Meiji-jingu in Tokyo, or Kenroku-en in Kanazawa.

07 Cosmos
(late Aug–early Oct)
Dot the rural landscape. Try Hama-rikyu in Tokyo and around Mt Fuji, particularly Yamanaka-ko.

08 Chrysanthemum
(Sep–mid-Nov)
The best place to see this symbol of Japan's Imperial Family is at Shinjuku-gyoen in Tokyo.

09 Autumn foliage
(late Nov–early Dec)
Coloured maples can be seen throughout the hillsides nationwide. Yellow gingko line the boulevards of many major cities.

10 Winter peonies
(late Nov–mid-Feb)
For a bit of colour in the winter season, try Ueno-koen or Hama-rikyu in Tokyo.

01 APHOTOSTORY/SHUTTERSTOCK ©, 02 M88/SHUTTERSTOCK ©, 03 STEPHANE BIDOUZE/SHUTTERSTOCK ©, 04 DREAMNIKON/SHUTTERSTOCK ©, 05 JUNJUN/SHUTTERSTOCK ©, 06 YURI-SS/SHUTTERSTOCK ©, 07 JREIKA/SHUTTERSTOCK ©, 08 KOJIRO/SHUTTERSTOCK ©, 09 P_WON/SHUTTERSTOCK ©, 10 NELLA/SHUTTERSTOCK ©

18

Zen & **BEYOND**

MONUMENTS | GARDENS | RELIGION

To many, the name Kyoto is synonymous with Zen. The city is home to over 1600 Buddhist temples (and 400 Shinto shrines), many internationally renowned for their gardens and architecture, and to visit them all would require a number of lifetimes.

🗺 **How to**

Getting around A relatively flat city, Kyoto is ideal for cycling or walking. Many of the sights are in clusters, so your visit can be broken into zones. Consider getting a Kansai Thru Pass if using public transport to go further afield.

Top tip Some temples are only open in certain seasons, while others offer a nighttime 'light-up' once or twice a year. Check the listings of the *Kyoto Visitor's Guide* for dates and times.

Temple Visiting

Where to start? Kyoto's real beauty lies in its religious sites, and your visit will inevitably revolve around them. While the major places can be crowded, they're still worth a visit, and are quietest an hour or two after opening, or late in the afternoon. Multiple-day visits to the city are a must, enabling you to explore specific corners. Try to pace yourself and don't schedule too many sites in a day, as some visitors find themselves getting templed-out.

With the Buddhas Kyoto's poster child is inevitably **Kinkaku-ji** (Golden Pavilion), famous not only for the eponymous villa standing regally above a reflective pond, but for its stroll garden of water and moss. A short walk away is **Ryoan-ji**, famed for

🏯 Votive Art

People write wishes and prayers on *ema* (little wooden plaques) and hang them around Shinto shrine grounds to be received by the gods. Colourful designs – traditionally horses or deities, but more recently anime characters or cultural icons – decorate the front.

Above left Kinkaku-ji (Golden Pavilion).
Above right *Ema.*
Left Ryoan-ji rock garden.

its deceptively simple courtyard garden of sand and stone. The two temples are absolutely magical on a snowy day. The stroll garden above **Ginkaku-ji** (Silver Pavilion) offers terrific views across town before you descend to be bathed in the scent of incense and seasonal flowers. Continue down the Path of Philosophy's quiet canal to **Nanzen-ji**, unmissable due to its towering gate.

Among the gods The face of the stroll garden behind **Heian-jingu** changes with whatever is in bloom. To walk beneath the 30,000 red gates of **Fushimi Inari-Taisha** has become the centrepiece to every visit, and the crowds prove it. (To be amidst the 2.7 million visitors during New Year's is an experience in itself.) On a pre-dawn visit, it will be just you and the gods.

Smaller Treasures

Visitors feeling pressured by the dictates of social media tend to focus on the A-listers, but be sure to visit a few of the quieter, lesser

🏯 Zen Meditation

One of Kyoto's most attractive experiences is a meditation session at a Zen temple. Since Kyoto temples tend to be of the Rinzai school of Zen, the participant sits facing the centre of the room, after finding a comfortable cross-legged position atop a round cushion. Soften your gaze to look 1.5m ahead, and rather than control thoughts, watch them come and go. And don't worry, receiving a whack from the stick of enlightenment is optional. Meditation sessions at **Bishamondo Shorin-ji** and **Kennin-ji** prove popular, while those at **Taizo-in** and **Shunko-in** are held in English.

119

Left Ginkaku-ji (Silver Pavilion).
Below Daitoku-ji.

LEFT: PIGPROX/SHUTTERSTOCK ©
RIGHT: COWARDLION/SHUTTERSTOCK ©

known sites too. Even better, stumble across your own. Compared to the big names, these will have modest entry fees and you may have the place to yourself.

At **Daitoku-ji**, the subtemple of **Koto-in**, is a riot of colour in autumn, and offers a contemplative respite for most of the year. Higashiyama's 36 peaks serve as borrowed scenery at **Shoden-ji**, hovering above a pristine rock garden. Nearby **Entsu-ji** presents a similar effect, though in this case the mountainscape is emulated within the garden moss. Visitors entering **Murin-an** villa, may feel the surrounding city drop away, before disappearing completely during the walk along the Kurodani/ Yoshida hill.

In a city this culturally rich, it's easy to find your own treasure. Aim towards the little oases of green among the city centre and you'll find a quiet time-out to rest your tired feet and overstimulated brain. In strolling the hilly edges of town, you'll inevitably come across the sprawling grounds of some of Kyoto's majestic, but little-visited, holy sites.

19 Strolling Through SAGA

WALKING | NATURE | CULTURE

▬▬▬ Wander this lesser-known corner of town, along rural lanes lined with thatch houses, popping into the lush grounds of temples along the way. Skirt the edge of the renowned bamboo forest, before lunching beside Katsura-gawa's quick-moving water.

7MARU/SHUTTERSTOCK©

🗺 Trip Notes

Getting there JR runs a frequent rail service to Saga Arashiyama from Kyoto Station. The most interesting approach is through the Kyoto suburbs on the little Keifuku Randen Arashiyama tram that departs from Omiya Station. Buses to Otagi-mae depart hourly from both Randen-Saga and Saga-Arashiyama Stations.

Top tip In summer, do this course in reverse and cross through a haunted tunnel to enjoy a swim beside Kiyotaki village.

🚶 Sleepy Sagano

This corner of Kyoto city is hardly city at all. There is a definitive rural feel in the thatched-roof teahouses, maple-infused temple grounds and family-run shops specialising in pottery and bamboo. Pleasantly free of crowds, this half-day walk serves as a refresher, before dropping down into buzzing Arashiyama.

01 The forested surroundings and unique architecture of **Otagi Nenbutsu-ji** take second stage to the hundreds of comically carved Buddhist Jizo statues.

02 Perhaps Kyoto's most atmospheric temple, **Gio-ji** has a moss landscape that's a subtle contrast of greens. It was founded by a former court dancer facing the impermanence of fading beauty.

03 **Okochi Sanso** is the former villa of Japan's most-loved silent film star. The path of it's stroll garden wends upward to offer fantastic views of Kyoto and the Katsura-gawa rushing below.

04 Take a different approach to the bamboo forest of **Arashiyama** to avoid the selfie-stick brigades. Continue through Kameyama-koen for riverside views.

05 The riverside veranda at **Kameyama-ya** overlooks forested hillsides and boaters. **Yoshimura** offers tasty soba noodles and good views of Togetsu-kyo bridge. Grab a coffee at **% Arabica**.

UKYO-KU

Osawa-no-ike

Okura-ike

Kameyama-koen

% Arabica

Yoshimura

Sanjo-dori

Kameyama-ya

Nakanoshima-koen

Arashiyama Monkey Park Iwatayama

500 m
0.25 miles

SEAONWEB/SHUTTERSTOCK ©. SEAN PAVONE/SHUTTERSTOCK ©

20 An Audience with the
DAIBUTSU

BUDDHISM | ARCHITECTURE | CULTURE

Visiting the Daibutsu (Great Buddha) of Todai-ji is the highlight of any trip to Nara. The serene face of the 15m-tall bronze has radiated calm for centuries, seemingly at odds with its imposing size. And how could one not feel peace under the gently curved roof of one of the world's largest and most beautiful wooden buildings.

B-HIDE THE SCENE/SHUTTERSTOCK ©

How to

Getting here Todai-ji is a 25-minute walk from JR Nara Station or 15 minutes from Kintetsu Nara Station. Alternatively, frequently departing buses run to Nara-koen for ¥220.

When to go Todai-ji is open year-round, from 7.30am to 5.30pm April to October, 8am to 5pm November to March. Mornings, particularly on weekends and holidays, are especially busy.

Top tip Visit before 9am or in the late afternoon to avoid the coach tours.

LUCIANO MORTULA - LGM/SHUTTERSTOCK ©

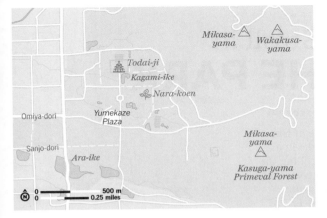

Above right Daibutsu, Todai-ji.
Below right Daibutsu-den.

The building A pair of 12th-century, 7m-tall wooden Nio (guardian) statues greet you on the approach to the World Heritage Daibutsu-den, which stands majestically against the nearby hills. Commissioned by the emperor to bring peace, the temple took two million workers over 15 years to complete.It was finally consecrated in 752 after nearly bankrupting the nation. The current structure, rebuilt in 1709, is two-thirds the size of the original.

The Buddha The 15m-high Daibutsu, cast in 749 from over 500 tons of bronze, has been frequently reconstructed in this land of earthquakes and fires. The body of the current statue dates to 1185, while the 5m-high head was recast in 1692. The right hand is held upright to dispel fear and to offer divine protection. Recent X-rays showed jewels, swords and even a human tooth inside the Buddha's knee.

The scene Most visitors find themselves drawn immediately to the Buddha, but take a moment to detour to the left and admire the red-faced statue of Binzuru, the Buddha's alcoholic doctor, with the wood rubbed away by worshippers seeking to heal the corresponding body part. Have a look behind the Buddha at models of the original temple site, noting the use of intricate wooden joints rather than nails. The hall's most lively attraction is a pillar with a hole in its base the same size as the Daibutsu's nostril. Giggling (or more often, grunting) visitors attempt to squeeze through so as to earn enlightenment in their next life.

🎋 Festivals

Yamayaki (Fire Festival) This mid-January event to burn away Wakakusa-yama's dead grass dates to 1760.

Mantoro (Lantern Festival) In Nara's most picturesque festival, Kasuga Taisha's 3000 lanterns are lit on 3 February, and again in mid-August.

Shikayose (Deer Calling) Nara-koen opened in 1862 with the blowing of a horn and this is recreated daily, with deer gathering around the horn player at Tobihino along the road to Kasuga Taisha.

Shuni-e Ceremony (Fire Festival) On 14 March, monks parade massive torches along the veranda of Nigatsu-do, raining embers on the crowd to purify them.

Shika-no-Tsunokiri (Antler Cutting) Nara-koen's deer are pursued into the Roku-en (deer enclosure) where their antlers are sawn off.

A Stroll in
THE PARK

NATURE | HISTORY | ARCHITECTURE

The compact nature of Nara-koen enables visitors to take in a number of sights while strolling the surfaced paths through the verdant green beneath Wakakusa-yama, accompanied by resident deer.

How to

Getting here Nara-koen is a 15-minute walk from JR Nara Station or five minutes from Kintetsu Nara Station. Alternatively, frequent buses run to the park for ¥220.

When to go Weekends and holidays are especially busy, but quiet is easy to find within the park's 660 hectares.

Top tip Festival days are particularly interesting, but be prepared for crowds.

Into the woods The highlights of Nara-koen should take one unhurried day. Starting at **Todai-ji** (p122), move clockwise through the park to return to the train station, and perhaps enjoy dinner or a drink on Sanjo-dori.

Natural treasures A gently sloping path brings you to **Nigatsu-do**, which in late winter is awash in flame at the **Shuni-e Ceremony** (p123). Founded in 752, the temple's main hall is a National Treasure. Views from the veranda look out over the city, with Todai-ji silhouetted massively against the distant Ikoma mountains. Follow the path along the base of Wakakusa-yama, where hill-dwelling

Above right Deer, Nara-koen.
Below right Kasuga Taisha.

BENNY MARTY/SHUTTERSTOCK ©

🏯 O-deer

Nara-koen's 1500 deer are a highlight in themselves. According to legend, the deity of Kasuga Taisha rode into the park on a white stag. Deer also symbolise the Buddha's most essential teachings. As such, they were considered sacred, and until 1637, it was a capital offence to kill one.

deer hobnob with their park-life cousins. Descend to **Kasuga Taisha**, an ancient site festooned with 3000 lanterns. You'll intuitively understand Shinto's nature-based ethic when strolling the quiet sub-shrines within the forest.

Among giants Follow the lantern-lined path to the **Nara National Museum**. The 1889 stone building houses a tremendous collection of Buddhist art, with many exhibits dating to the 8th century. Strolling across the grounds of the adjacent **Kofuku-ji**, you'll pass Japan's second-tallest wooden pagoda, and the unique Octagonal Hall at the far end of the courtyard. Descend the steps here to **Sarusawa-ike** pond.

VLADIMIR ZHOGA/SHUTTERSTOCK ©

22 The Walk that
SPANS TIME

HISTORY | WALKING | DAY TRIP

Yamanobe-no-michi is Japan's oldest road and one of its most picturesque. This three- to four-hour walk takes in 15 centuries of history, from the tombs of ancient emperors to kiosks selling healthy goodies harvested this very week.

B.S.P.I./GETTY IMAGES ©

🗺 Trip Notes

Getting there Frequent trains leave JR Nara Station for the short 13-minute ride to Tenri. A 30-minute walk brings you to start of the Yamanobe-no-michi, through a quaint shopping arcade lost in time, and past the massive temple complex of the Tenrikyo, one of the largest of Japan's new religions.

Top tip While this walk can be undertaken year-round, autumn allows you the opportunity to weigh yourself down with the region's famous persimmons.

⚓ Sake & Noodles

One of Japan's oldest shrines, **Omiwa-jinja** is not only the official shrine of sake brewing but also the birthplace of *somen* (thin wheat-flour noodles). Both can be enjoyed at the end of your walk, at one of the numerous cafes between the shrine and Miwa Station.

01 Cockerels freely roam the grounds of **Isonokami-jingu**, one of Japan's oldest shrines, and are a symbolic link not only to the sun goddess, but to the 'bird-perch' *torii* (entrance gate).

02 Friendly and earthy **Cafe Wawa Tenri** is the perfect rest stop for a cup of coffee, a slow-cooked lunch or even to try your hand at fruit-picking.

03 Walls of packed earth and tile lead you through the settlement of **Takenouchi**, whose moats have been keeping the villagers from enemies since the 16th century.

04 **Chogakuji**, nestled against the hills, has a lovely garden and the oldest wooden bell tower gate in Japan. The restaurant has been serving *somen* since 1783.

05 Birdlife is rife on the pond that surrounds the largest of the region's many burial mounds, including the 250m-wide tomb of **Emperor Sujin**, one of Japan's earliest rulers.

EBIQ/GETTY IMAGES ©
JOHN S LANDER/LIGHTROCKET VIA GETTY IMAGES ©

N 0   1 km
   0   0.5 miles

Listings

BEST OF THE REST

Natural Escapes

Hiei-zan

Kyoto is notorious for its sweltering summer, so head for a cooling walk beneath towering cedars, amongst the Enryaku-ji buildings spread throughout the forest.

Isshu Trail

Descend from the overlook above Fushimi Inari-Taisha's red gates down the Kyoto Isshu Trail. Make your way toward Tofuku-ji's famous temples, passing stone gods that flank hidden waterfalls.

Kyoto Botanical Gardens

One of the city's less-visited gems, with 12,000 species of plants offering a wide display of seasonal colours, a bustling avian community and lush paths perfect for strolling.

Imperial Palace Grounds

Former home to the Imperial family, this 100-hectare park at the centre of the city is one of the best places to let the kids work off excess energy.

Daimonji-yama

Undertake the one-hour climb up this mountain's kanji-carved face to watch the setting sun light up the temple roofs below as well as Osaka's far-off skyscrapers.

◎ Pulses of the City

Fushimi Sake Village   ¥¥¥

The spirit(s) of Fushimi, Japan's second-largest sake district, is honoured at this restaurant that offers a sampler of each of the town's 18 breweries. A food accompaniment is highly advised.

Gekkeikan Sake Okura Museum

Perhaps the gem of the Fushimi district, this museum guides you through the making of its famous sake, topped off with a tasting. You even get a complimentary one for the train home.

Kyoto Taiko Center

Find the heartbeat of Japan by having a go at playing *taiko*, traditional Japanese festival drums. Held within the hall of Chomyo-ji temple, you will surely rouse the deities.

Kyoto Sights & Nights

Enjoy a walking lecture around Kyoto's geisha districts led by an expert on geisha culture. Also available are drinks with a *maiko* or a geisha dinner party.

✒ Dine-in

Nishiki Market   ¥

Graze as you go, sampling many of the facets of Kyoto's internationally renowned food culture. A mere five blocks long, Nishiki's hundreds of shops offers everything from octopus skewers to tofu doughnuts.

Octopus skewer, Nishiki Market.

BOOKIEAKAITCH/SHUTTERSTOCK ©

Dragon Burger ¥

Chef Adam Rawson created his award-winning burgers with the Japanese palate in mind. Try a sampler of wasabi burger, *yuzu-kosho* burger and cacao BBQ sliders, along with a local beer.

Dining room you ¥¥¥

Tucked away in a quiet neighbourhood, you is a subdued introduction to *izakaya* culture. Best known for its *obanzai-ryori* (home-style cooking) and seasonal oysters, and for its vast choice of sakes.

Ganko Nijo-en ¥¥

The Kiyamachi location of the popular franchise is set within an L-shaped 1611 villa with a spacious garden and a quieter vibe than the usual *izakaya*.

Men-Bistro Nakano ¥¥

This unique shop serves ramen with a French vibe. The original flavour of the soup infers the chef's training in continental cuisine. Not to mention the fine selection of wines.

Pontocho Karyu ¥¥¥

The best choice for *yuka* dining, eaten above a cooling stream for a respite from Kyoto's relentless summer heat.

🛍 Souvenirs & Treasures

Robert Yellin Yakimono Gallery

Marvel at the diversity that pottery can take at this picturesque gallery, run by one of the top foreign experts of Japanese ceramics. Be sure to email or call before visiting.

Hakuchikudo

For those visiting in the heat of summer, a folding fan is a must. Choose from the artistic treasures at the Hakuchikudo atelier, which has been making fans since 1717.

JENJ PAYLESS2/SHUTTERSTOCK ©

Nara City Museum of Photography.

Shogo-in Yatsuhashi Sohonten Kyoto

Born in 1689, the sweet bean-filled cinnamon confectionery known as *yatsuhashi* has gone on to become one of the city's favourite edible souvenirs. Also try the uncooked *cannelle* style.

Funahashiya

The speciality of this charming centuries-old shop near Sanjo Bridge are the dried-bean candies called *goshiki-mame*, sold in an array of flavours such as *yuzu* (citrus), cinnamon and plum.

🏛 Around the Perimeter

Nara City Museum of Photography

Hidden behind the modern facade is a collection of over 1000 Meiji and Taisho period photographs, as well as a 50-year documentation of Nara festivals and everyday life.

Shiga Naoya House

One of Japan's eminent novelists spent a decade in this modest home beside Nara-koen. This well-preserved blend of East and West centres on a lush garden.

Scan for more things to see, do and try in Kyoto & Nara

OSAKA

FOOD | CITY LIFE | SIGHTS

Experience Osaka online

FUJIFOTO/GETTY IMAGES ©

Yodo-gawa

Get amazing night-time views over the city from the floating garden at the top of the **Umeda Sky Building** (p144)
🕐 *1–2 hours*

UMEDA

SHINCHI

Tosabori-gawa

NAKA-NO-
SHIMA

SEMBA

Aji-gawa

OSAKA
Trip Builder

Stroll through the quiet alleyways of **Hozen-ji Yokocho** (p139)
🕐 *1–2 hours*

Japan's 'second' city and food capital, Osaka has all the trappings of a modern megalopolis in an area more compact than Tokyo, with a rougher edge and charm to boot. A must for street food, bright lights and shopping heaven.

Dotombori-gawa

DOTOMBORI

Explore bookable experiences in Osaka online

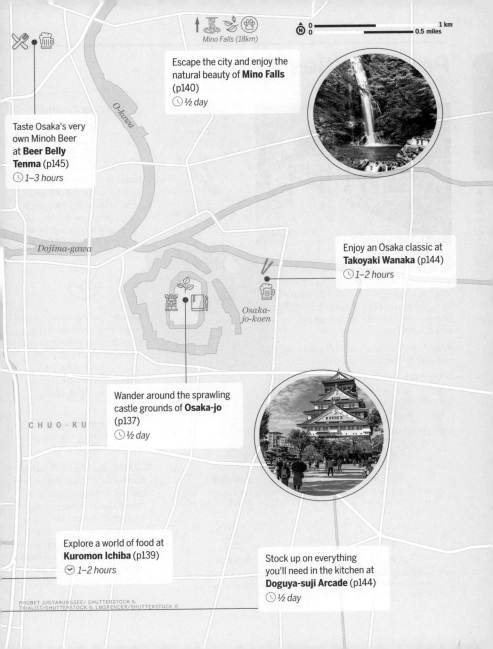

Mino Falls (18km)

Taste Osaka's very own Minoh Beer at **Beer Belly Tenma** (p145)
🕐 1–3 hours

Escape the city and enjoy the natural beauty of **Mino Falls** (p140)
🕐 ½ day

O-kawa

Dojima-gawa

Enjoy an Osaka classic at **Takoyaki Wanaka** (p144)
🕐 1–2 hours

Osaka-jo-koen

Wander around the sprawling castle grounds of **Osaka-jo** (p137)
🕐 ½ day

CHUO-KU

Explore a world of food at **Kuromon Ichiba** (p139)
🕐 1–2 hours

Stock up on everything you'll need in the kitchen at **Doguya-suji Arcade** (p144)
🕐 ½ day

PHUBET JUNTARUNGSEE/ SHUTTERSTOCK ©, TRIALIST/SHUTTERSTOCK ©, LMSPENCER/SHUTTERSTOCK ©

Practicalities

CHINTUNG LEE/SHUTTERSTOCK ©

ARRIVING

Kansai International Airport Two train lines into the city: Nankai is best for Namba (40 minutes, ¥1500); JR for Osaka (Umeda) or Shin-Osaka (one hour, ¥2400). Buses cost ¥1600 and take about 90 minutes (kate.co.jp); taxis are very expensive (¥18,000).

Itami Airport Mostly handles domestic flights; a monorail connects with trains to the city.

Shin-Osaka Station If arriving by shinkansen (bullet train), change to the JR line for Osaka or the Mido-suji subway line to reach downtown.

HOW MUCH FOR A

Tray of takoyaki
¥600

Bowl of ramen
¥750

Craft beer
¥800

GETTING AROUND

Train The JR loop line is useful for accessing most of Osaka's main areas, with major stops including Osaka (Umeda), Kyobashi, Tennoji and some trains to JR Namba Station.

S

Subway The Osaka metro has many lines, the most handy for visitors being the Mido-suji (red) line which runs north–south between Shin-Osaka, Umeda, Shinsaibashi, Namba and Tennoji stations.

IC Card Osaka's top-up transport card is called ICOCA and saves the hassle of buying tickets for every journey. It can be used throughout Kansai (and also in Tokyo) for trains (both JR and private lines), subways and some buses. Buy at JR ticket machines (preload with ¥2000, including a ¥500 refundable deposit).

WHEN TO GO

MAR–MAY
Warm in the day, cool at night; cherry blossoms peak in early April

JUN–AUG
Rainy season from June to mid-July, then stiflingly hot and humid

SEP–NOV
Hot until October;, autumn colours from late November

DEC–FEB
Cold and dry; most places close a few days around New Year

EATING & DRINKING

Best areas There are great places to eat and drink all across the city, although Umeda and especially Namba tend to be the first stops for restaurants and bars. Other foodie districts include Fukushima (ramen), Tsuruhashi (Korea town and *yakiniku* capital), and Tenma with its labyrinth of lively back-alley restaurants and famous Tenjinbashi-suji.

Specialities Osaka's signature dishes are *takoyaki* (fried octopus balls) and *okonomiyaki* (a kind of cabbage pancake), hearty soul foods made from a batter base.

Must-try ramen
Menya Joroku (p144)

Best okonomiyaki
Ajinoya Honten (p139)

CONNECT & FIND YOUR WAY

Wi-fi There is free wi-fi in some areas (ofw-oer.com/en).

Navigation Osaka is divided into two main areas: Umeda or Kita (north) centres on JR Osaka Station, while Minami (south) comprises the bustling downtown districts of Namba, Shinsaibashi and Dotombori. There are large tourist information centres in JR Osaka Station, and on the 1st floor of Nankai Namba Station.

DISCOUNT CARDS

Osaka Amazing Pass Enables unlimited use of trains and buses, plus entry to numerous attractions and discounts in some restaurants and shops (osaka-info.jp).

WHERE TO STAY

There are many accommodation options across the city, especially around Umeda and Namba, ranging from budget hostels and capsule hotels to fancy five-star establishments.

Neighbourhood	Pro/Con
Namba	Great for food, entertainment and nightlife, but also big crowds.
Umeda	Busy transit hub with plenty of shopping and dining options.
Tennoji	Good train links if slightly out of the way. Near some of Osaka's seedier neighbourhoods.
Honmachi	Central location, but much quieter and less going on than either Namba or Umeda, especially at night.
Shin-Osaka	Great for the shinkansen and close to Umeda. Hotels and restaurants, but not much else.
Osaka-jo	Some hotels within walking distance of the castle and park; generally very quiet.

MONEY

Always carry a good wad of notes as although cashless payment is becoming more common, not everywhere accepts cards (especially smaller businesses and restaurants). Travel cards and passes can save you money.

TOP: KALI0ZZ/SHUTTERSTOCK ©

23 Exploring THE CITY

CITY WALK | SIGHTSEEING | LANDMARKS

OSAKA EXPERIENCES

━━━ This half- to full-day walking tour takes in most of Osaka's main sights and interesting neighbourhoods which best showcase the lively vibe of the city, with plenty of opportunities for food and rest stops.

MIRKO KUZMANOVIC/ALAMY STOCK PHOTO ©

🗺 Trip Notes

Getting around The full walk covers at least 6.5km, but it's possible to hop on and off the train or subway anywhere.

When to go Year-round, although summer (July, August and early September) is hot.

Highlight Hit Dotombori in the evening to see the riverside lights at their neon best.

Top tip If you don't fancy walking, rent a bicycle – check hubchari.com for rentals across the city.

❄ Time Your Trip

Early April is **hanami** (cherry-blossom viewing) season and Osaka-jo is one of the best spots to enjoy it.

Check out the fantastic **flea market** at Shitennoji on the 21st and 22nd of every month. The Nipponbashi Street Festa is a **cosplay festival** held each March in Den Den Town.

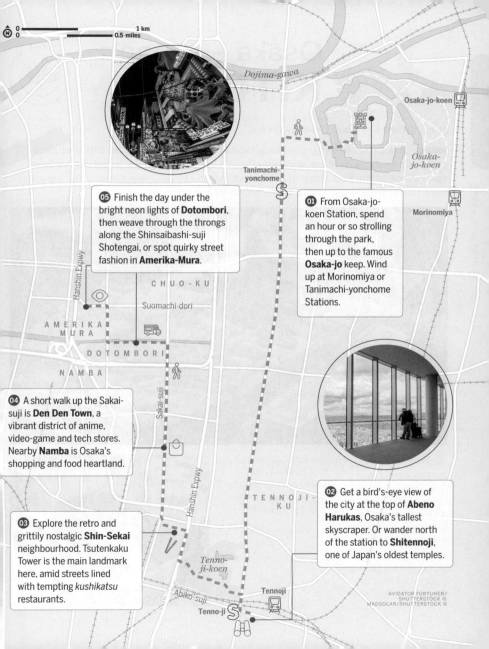

05 Finish the day under the bright neon lights of **Dotombori**, then weave through the throngs along the Shinsaibashi-suji Shotengai, or spot quirky street fashion in **Amerika-Mura**.

01 From Osaka-jo-koen Station, spend an hour or so strolling through the park, then up to the famous **Osaka-jo** keep. Wind up at Morinomiya or Tanimachi-yonchome Stations.

04 A short walk up the Sakai-suji is **Den Den Town**, a vibrant district of anime, video-game and tech stores. Nearby **Namba** is Osaka's shopping and food heartland.

02 Get a bird's-eye view of the city at the top of **Abeno Harukas**, Osaka's tallest skyscraper. Or wander north of the station to **Shitennoji**, one of Japan's oldest temples.

03 Explore the retro and grittily nostalgic **Shin-Sekai** neighbourhood. Tsutenkaku Tower is the main landmark here, amid streets lined with tempting *kushikatsu* restaurants.

N

1 km
0.5 miles

Dojima-gawa

Osaka-jo-koen

Osaka-jo-koen

Tanimachi-yonchome

Morinomiya

Hanshin Expwy

CHUO-KU

Suomachi-dori

AMERIKA MURA

DOTOMBORI

NAMBA

Sakai-suji

Hanshin Expwy

TENNOJI-KU

Tennoji-koen

Tennoji

Abiko-suji

Tenno-ji

AVIGATOR FORTUNER/
SHUTTERSTOCK ©
MADSOLAR/SHUTTERSTOCK ©

24 Osaka – Japan's KITCHEN

FOOD | MARKET | LOCAL SPECIALITIES

Osaka is a city with a serious food obsession, summed up with the local expression *kuidaore* – 'eat until you drop'. Great food can be found everywhere, and so one of the best ways to explore the city is by following your eyes, ears and nose to discover some of the most mouth-watering bites.

YULIA GRIGORYEVA/SHUTTERSTOCK ©

📍 How to

Getting around Most of Osaka is very walkable, and you can eat and drink until late as the trains and subways run until around midnight.

When to go Year-round, although many establishments close for a few days around New Year.

Fun fact Cup ramen (pot noodles) and *kaiten-zushi* (conveyor-belt sushi) were both invented in Osaka.

PAKONG/SHUTTERSTOCK ©

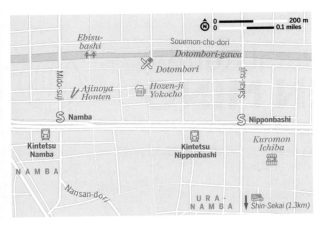

Downtown dishes The bright lights and lively buzz of **Dotombori** make it Osaka's most popular hangout spot, especially around the famous **Ebisu-bashi** bridge and giant Glico 'running man' sign. The streets are lined with *takoyaki* vendors, ramen bars and a barrage of colourful shops and signage, so grab some street food and soak up the sights and sounds. The area is also chockful of restaurants – just south of the bridge, **Ajinoya Honten** is one of the best places for *okonomiyaki*, while the atmospheric and old-fashioned cobbled alleyways of **Hozen-ji Yokocho** are home to cosy *izakayas* (Japanese pub-eateries) which come alive at night.

Food shopping At the heart of Osaka's culinary scene, **Kuromon Ichiba** (Kuromon Market) is home to numerous stores selling fresh seafood, meat, fruit, vegetables and sweets – many have stalls out front which cook food on the spot. A few blocks west is **Sennichimae Doguyasuji**, a covered shopping street dedicated to kitchenware, with great foodie souvenirs.

Deep-fried delights An early-20th-century Osaka invention, *kushikatsu* is skewered meat, seafood and vegetables coated in breadcrumbs, deep fried and served with a dark, tangy dipping sauce. The antiquated and charmingly shabby streets of **Shin-Sekai** are rammed with *kushikatsu* restaurants, so take your pick and enjoy with a cold beer.

Above left Kuromon Ichiba.
Below left *Kushikatsu*.

Local Specialities

Osaka is called the 'nation's kitchen' because as a merchant city it became a literal storehouse of goods, like a kitchen in the home – while in culinary terms the city is known for its hearty local dishes.

Takoyaki is Osaka's most famous street food; these golf-ball-size dollops of hot gooey batter are stuffed with octopus (*tako*) and cooked until crispy on the outside, then topped with a savoury sauce, mayonnaise, powdered seaweed and bonito fish flakes.

Okonomiyaki is another Osaka staple – savoury pancakes crammed with shredded cabbage and your choice of meat, seafood and vegetables, often cooked at your table.

25 Rural Retreat
IN MINO

WALK | NATURE | WATERFALL

███████ Osaka isn't all bright lights and big crowds – the rural outpost of Mino is only 25 minutes from Umeda by train, and offers gentle woodland walks to a scenic waterfall, with the chance of spotting wild monkeys en route. Beautiful in any season, it's also home to one of Japan's best-known craft beer breweries.

🧭 **How to**

Getting here From Hankyu Osaka-Umeda Station take a train on the Hankyu Takarazuka line to Ishibashi Handai-Mae Station, then transfer to the Hankyu Mino line and get off at the last stop.

When to go All year, but especially popular around late November for the autumn colours.

Take note Mino is also sometimes anglicised as 'Minoo' or 'Minoh'.

Map:
- 0 — 5 km
- 0 — 2.5 miles
- *Meiji-no-mori Mino Quasi National Park*
- *Mino Falls*
- Kawanishi
- Ikeda
- Itami
- Toyonaka
- Suita
- Nishinomiya
- Osaka

Walk in the woods Clearly signposted from the station, the walk begins with a stroll up a narrow street lined with small shops and restaurants. Then follow a pretty riverside course through the forest, passing Ryuan-ji, a small woodland temple, before winding up at the impressive 33m tall **Mino Falls** in 45 minutes. The gentle 3km route is paved from start to finish, with numerous hiking trails heading deeper into the hills for the more adventurous.

Nature calls Despite its close proximity to the city, Mino is a haven for wildlife, most notably the Japanese

Above right Mino Falls.
Below right Japanese macaque.

🍺 Beer Belly

Established in 1997, Minoh Beer was one of Japan's first microbreweries and is now arguably the country's most famous craft beer, with bottles in almost every shop in the area. The best place to quench your thirst is the Minoh Beer Warehouse, a 20-minute walk southeast of Mino Station.

macaque – groups of these primates can often be seen wandering near the path, and although somewhat accustomed to humans they should not be fed. Other creatures to keep an eye out for include wild boar, deer and numerous bird species. The Mino Park Insectarium is also worth a visit if you like creepy-crawlies.

Autumnal attractions
Around late November is *koyo* (the coming of autumn colours) and Mino is one of Osaka's most popular leaf-viewing spots, as the forests become a vivid blaze of red, yellow and orange. It is also the best time to sample a Mino delicacy, *momiji tempura* (deep-fried maple leaves), sold by vendors and at shops along the trail.

Tastes of **JAPAN**

01 Sushi
Vinegared rice topped with raw fish and sometimes wrapped in *nori* (seaweed), served with soy sauce and wasabi.

02 Ramen
Wheat noodles in a rich broth from a meat or fish-based stock. Toppings include sliced braised pork, vegetables and eggs.

03 Udon
Thick white noodles made from wheat flour, usually served in a light broth with a variety of toppings.

04 Soba
Thin noodles made from buckwheat, either eaten cold with a dipping sauce, wasabi and scallions, or in a hot broth.

05 Yakiniku
Literally meaning 'grilled meat', slices of beef or pork cooked on a charcoal grill, eaten with rice and dipping sauces.

06 Japanese curry
Generally sweet and mild rather than eye-wateringly spicy. Also called *kare-raisu* (curry rice), it is eaten with a spoon.

07 Nabe

A broad term for meat/seafood and vegetables cooked in a hotpot; variations include *shabu-shabu* and sukiyaki.

08 Yakitori

Bite-size pieces of chicken on a skewer, cooked over charcoal and seasoned with salt or a *tare* (sauce).

09 Kushikatsu

Small pieces of meat, seafood and vegetables skewered, then battered in panko bread crumbs and deep-fried, then dipped in a dark sauce.

10 Tonkatsu

Pork cutlet coated in breadcrumbs and deep-fried, served with rice, shredded cabbage and a tangy tonkatsu sauce.

11 Tempura

Thinly sliced meat, seafood or vegetables covered in a light and crispy batter, sometimes eaten with a dipping sauce.

12 Okonomiyaki

A savoury pancake made of a wheat-flour batter mixed with cabbage, meat or seafood, and cooked on a *teppan* (iron hotplate).

01 NIPAPORN PANYACHAROEN/SHUTTERSTOCK ©. 02 KRAVTZOV/SHUTTERSTOCK ©. 03 CATINSYRUP/GETTY IMAGES ©. 04 ARANCIO/SHUTTERSTOCK, 05 WPIXZ/SHUTTERSTOCK ©. 06 KARIPHOTO/SHUTTERSTOCK ©. 07 ARTIT WONGPRADU/SHUTTERSTOCK ©. 08 FUNNY FACE/SHUTTERSTOCK ©. 09 JREIKA/SHUTTERSTOCK ©. 10 FUNNY FACE/SHUTTERSTOCK ©. 11 SASASAWA/SHUTTERSTOCK ©. 12 BONCHAN/SHUTTERSTOCK ©

Listings

BEST OF THE REST

◎ Popular Attractions

Universal Studios Japan

Popular theme park 10 minutes by train from Osaka Station. Rides and attractions for all ages, including Harry Potter– and Super Nintendo–themed worlds. Can get busy, so avoid weekends and holidays.

Umeda Sky Building

An Umeda landmark, two 40-storey towers connected at the top by a large observatory and outdoor viewing deck offering great night-time city views. A 15-minute walk from JR Osaka Station.

Osaka Aquarium Kaiyukan

One of the largest aquariums in Japan, 30 minutes by train from central Osaka. See a staggering array of fish and other marine life including sea otters, penguins and whale sharks.

Sumiyoshi Taisha

Founded in the 3rd century, Sumiyoshi Taisha is one of the oldest shrines in Japan and famous for its beautifully arched red bridge. Just 10 minutes by train south of Namba.

Osaka Museum of Housing & Living

Spend an hour or two exploring detailed and evocative recreations of streets and buildings from yesteryear Osaka at this compact but fascinating museum, located directly above Tenjimbashisuji 6-chome Station.

Doguya-suji Arcade

This long arcade sells just about anything related to the preparation, consumption and selling of Osaka's principal passion – food. There's everything from bamboo steamers and lacquer miso soup bowls to shopfront lanterns, plastic food models and, of course, moulded hotplates for making *takoyaki*.

⫽ Soul Food & Noodle Dishes

Okonomiyaki Mizuno   ¥

A popular place for *okonomiyaki* that has been making Osaka's signature dish since 1945, so they know what they're doing. Located halfway between Namba and Nipponbashi metro stations.

Takoyaki Wanaka   ¥

It's not hard to find *takoyaki* in Osaka, but this well-known chain serves up crispy yet delightfully gooey-on-the-inside octopus balls. Quick and friendly service. There's a branch in Osaka-jo park.

Menya Joroku   ¥

Celebrated ramen shop in Namba, specialising in bowls using a rich chicken-based stock. Don't miss the *chuka soba*, their signature soy-sauce ramen. Small place so there's usually a queue, but worth it.

Osaka Museum of Housing & Living.

OCHIVIS PICTURES/SHUTTERSTOCK ©

Ramen Jinsei JET ¥

Popular ramen restaurant a short walk north of JR Fukushima Station, serving hearty bowls of chicken ramen in a thick broth. Order from the vending machine outside (staff can help).

Dotombori Imai Honten ¥¥

An oasis of calm among the downtown hubbub, this udon restaurant one minute from Ebisu-bashi bridge is a long-running Osaka institution known for its top-notch food and old-style ambience.

🍴 Sushi & Seafood

Genrokuzushi ¥

The first *kaiten-zushi* (conveyor-belt sushi) in the world, now with restaurants across the city – the Sennichimae branch is probably the best. Decent, affordable sushi and English menus.

Junchan Sushi ¥¥

Tucked away in a quiet corner of Dotombori, this small and friendly sushi place serves big, fresh portions but is reasonably priced. Try the *omakase* (chef's selection) set. Reservations are sometimes required.

Endo Sushi ¥¥

Amazingly fresh top-grade sushi at this family-run restaurant next to Osaka Central Wholesale Fish Market. Popular with locals and tourists; expect to wait even early in the morning. Cash only.

🍺 Craft Beer & Bars

Beer Belly Tenma ¥¥

Flagship branch with a long bar and large selection of Osaka's own Minoh Beer, including stouts and IPAs. Located in the bustling rabbit warren of restaurants just north of JR Tenma Station.

Umeda Sky Building.

HIROSHI H/SHUTTERSTOCK ©

Craft Beer Base Bud ¥¥

Hidden deep under Osaka Station (floor BF2), this relaxed and friendly place serves a rotating mix of international and Japanese beers, plus good grub.

Yellow Ape Craft ¥¥

Wide beer selection, great food and friendly staff. Use a card to self-serve at over 15 taps, then pay at the end. New branch next to Yodoyabashi Station.

Music Bar Groovy ¥¥

Cosy atmosphere, cool tunes, quirky vintage decor and a friendly clientele of locals and foreigners. Situated right next to Dobutsuen-Mae Station (exit 8); the owner Wataru speaks great English.

Scan to find more things to see, do and try in Osaka

26 Day Trip to
HIMEJI-JO

HISTORY | CASTLE | WORLD HERITAGE

Known as the 'White Heron' or 'White Egret' thanks to its dazzling white exterior, Himeji-jo is Japan's most spectacular castle. Sitting perched on a hill overlooking Himeji, a small city on the coast of the Seto Inland Sea, Himeji-jo is easily accessed by rail and makes a great day trip from Osaka and Kyoto, or a convenient stop-off if heading further west.

ALEKSANDAR TODOROVIC/SHUTTERSTOCK ©

🗺 How to

Getting here 30 minutes (¥3280) from Shin-Osaka on the shinkansen or one hour from Osaka Station on JR Special Rapid trains. The castle is a 15-minute walk north of Himeji Station, or a five-minute bus ride (get off at Otemon-mae stop, ¥100).

When to go Open all year (except 29/30 December); avoid busy times such as weekends and national holidays.

How much ¥1000 for adults, ¥300 for under 18s, preschool children free.

CYRUS_2000/SHUTTERSTOCK ©

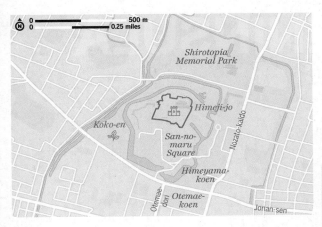

Above left Main tower, Himeji-jo.
Below left Interior, Himeji-jo.

Deep history Designated as a National Treasure and one of only 12 original castles remaining in Japan (most are modern reconstructions), Himeji-jo is famed for its magnificent form, size and maze-like castle grounds. The site has been home to fortifications since 1333, and the current castle was built in 1580 by Toyotomi Hideyoshi, enlarged 30 years later by Ikeda Terumasa, and was then home to generations of feudal lords. Himeji-jo saw little conflict, but has survived earthquakes and WWII bombings. The castle reopened in 2015 after five years of refurbishment; its walls and eaves were covered in traditional white plaster to restore the castle to its original beauty.

Explore the castle The grounds are divided by stone walls, gates, moats and other buildings and can be explored at leisure, while the seven floors of the towering main keep require you to take off your shoes (to protect the wooden floors) and clamber up multiple sets of excitingly steep and narrow stairs. The arrow-marked route through the castle takes about 1½ hours to complete, and the keep is inaccessible for wheelchairs and strollers.

Hidden surprises Keep your eyes peeled for lots of easy-to-miss details such as the various-shaped small openings for firing bows and guns, tiny hiding holes in the corners of the keep, and carved numbers and letters on wooden beams (used to aid construction).

🏯 Beyond the Castle

Just west of the castle is **Koko-en**, nine exquisitely reconstructed Edo-period homes and gardens, including the lord's residence (complete with pond and waterfall), a teahouse and a bamboo grove.

Many historical TV dramas have been filmed here, and it's a lovely place to sip *matcha* (powdered green tea) or enjoy a *bentō* (boxed meal) in peaceful surroundings. Entry is ¥310/150 for adults/children (¥1050/¥360 with combined castle ticket).

Be sure to try the Himeji speciality *anago* (conger eel); nowhere does it better than the small and smoky Yamayoshi near the station. Also on the menu at Kassui-ken in Koko-en.

KII PENINSULA

TEMPLES | HIKING | NATURE

**Experience
Kii Peninsula
online**

0 20 km
0 10 miles

KII PENINSULA
Trip Builder

Remote and mountainous, the Kii Peninsula has long been considered sacred ground, drawing the religious ascetics who established the monastery at Koya-san and the pilgrimage trails of the Kumano Kodo. This is a place to experience Japan's spiritual side.

Kuwana

Yokkaichi

Kameyama ● Suzuka

Tsu

Matsusaka

Ise

● Kishiwada

○ Sennan
Hashimoto
Gojo

Iwade
Kino-gawa
● Wakayama
Koya-san

○ Kainan

○ Arida

○ Yuasa

Kii Channel

○ Yura

Gobo

○ Inami

Ryujin

Totsukawa

Hongu

Chikatsu-yu

○ Tanabe

○ Shirahama

Hiki ○

Kumano

Shiko

Atawa

Shingu

Nachi-Katsuura

Taiji

Kushimoto

Owase

Hike part (or all) of the **Nakahechi Trail**, the main Kumano Kodo pilgrim path (p154)
🕐 1–5 days

Explore the wooded sanctuary **Oku-no-in** at Koya-san (p158)
🕐 1 day

Learn about Kumano Kodo history and culture at the **Kumano Hongu Heritage Centre** (p162)
🕐 2 hours

Soak in the healing waters of **Tsubo-yu** (p162)
🕐 ½ day

See the waterfall **Nachi-no-taki** and the shrine, Kumano Nachi Taisha, built to worship it (p162)
🕐 ½ day

Explore bookable experiences in the Kii Peninsula online

PAL TERAVAGIMOV/SHUTTERSTOCK ©, ACHIKOCHI/SHUTTERSTOCK © COWARDLION/SHUTTERSTOCK ©

Pacific Ocean

Practicalities

ARRIVING

Kansai International Airport At the top of the peninsula; convenient for Kii destinations.

Osaka Get express trains for Koya-san (nearest station: Gokurakubashi) and Kumano (nearest station: Tanabe).

FIND YOUR WAY

Community-based operator Kumano Travel (tb-kumano. jp) has lots of trip-planning resources for hiking the Kumano Kodo and handles bookings for inns.

MONEY

Book online and pay with a card for Kumano lodgings or carry a lot of cash, as there are no ATMs outside the gateway cities.

WHERE TO STAY

Place	Pro/Con
Koya-san	Stay in a temple lodge; convenient for Koya-san sights, but not others.
Tanabe	Western gateway to the Kumano Kodo. Convenient but limited options.
Hongu	Central base for exploring Kumano; the best options in the region.
Yunomine Onsen	Fewer options and less convenient then Hongu, but accommodation has hot-spring baths.

EATING & DRINKING

Restaurants in Koya-san and along the Kumano Kodo have limited hours (around 11am to 4pm), so get breakfast and dinner at your lodging. Kumano Kodo inns will prepare *bento* (boxed meals) for lunch on the trails at an extra cost (around ¥1000). *Shojin-ryori* (Buddhist vegetarian cuisine) and *goma-dofu* (sesame tofu) are Koya-san specialities.

Best goma-dofu
Hamadaya (p163)

Must-try snack
Onsen tamago (eggs cooked in hot-spring water)

GETTING AROUND

Bus Kii has a solid local bus network.

Cable car To reach Koya-san, take the cable car from Gokurakubashi.

Car Convenient for the sights if you don't plan to do much hiking; don't drive to Koya-san in winter as the mountain road can be dangerous.

TOP: BONCHAN/SHUTTERSTOCK ©
BOTTOM: YULIA LISITSA/GETTY IMAGES ©

KII PENINSULA FIND YOUR FEET

❄
JAN–MAR
Low season: fewer crowds, but short days, cold nights and closures

⛅
APR–JUN
Gradually warmer days and evenings

☀
JUL–SEP
Peak season for escaping the summer heat in the mountains

🌤
OCT–DEC
Popular time to visit for fall foliage in Kumano

27

In the Footsteps
OF PILGRIMS

HIKING | NATURE | CULTURE

The Kumano Kodo is a
network of trails deep in the
interior of the Kii Peninsula,
first mapped centuries ago
by mountain ascetics seeking
spiritual enlightenment. There
are gentle day hikes and more
serious treks, plus onsen, shrines
and scenic vistas.

🗺 How to

When to go It's possible to hike the Nakahechi route year-round, though bear in mind that you'll have fewer daylight hours to work with in winter, so plan accordingly (it's a good idea to have a headlamp).

Getting around You'll use a combination of legwork, buses and maybe a boat – how much of each is up to you. The Nakahechi Trail starts at Takijiri-oji, a 40-minute bus ride from Kii-Tanabe Station.

Shrines The great shrines of Kumano Hongu Taisha (p162), Kumano Hayatama Taisha (p162) and Kumano Nachi Taisha (p162) are the big draw for pilgrims on the trails; each is located at a deeply spiritual spot. The Nakahechi Trail runs between them, spanning (almost) the Kii Peninsula from west to east.

Planning your hike Most travellers access the trails via Tanabe (Kii-Tanabe Station), a small city on the west coast of the peninsula, and finish at one of the cities on the east coast, Shingu or Nachi-Katsuura (Kii-Katsuura Station). **Kumano Travel** has an office in Tanabe, which is a great place to get current trail information, pick up maps and bus schedules and meet other travellers; they can also arrange luggage storage and shipping.

🚶 The Kohechi Trail

Experienced hikers can tackle the Kohechi Trail, which runs between Koya-san and Hongu. It's 70km long, with major elevation changes, and typically done over four days, with overnights in Omata, Miura-guchi and Totsukawa Onsen. Only passable April to November.

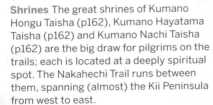

Above left Kumano Hongu Taisha (p162).
Above right Kumano Kodo trail guide.
Left Kumano Kodo.

Walking the Nakahechi Trail The trail is broken down into numerous sections, bookended by small settlements where there are simple guesthouses to spend the night and get hot meals. The settlements also join the road, and you can pick up the bus at each, and also at some 'oji' – small temples that function as trail markers. Clearly signposted in English, the well-maintained trail is a mix of paved paths, packed earth and stone worn smooth after centuries of pilgrims treading them; the latter can get quite slippery when wet – poles can be a good hedge for balance. There are public toilets every few kilometres.

Takijiri-oji to Hongu A good intro to the Nakahechi is the two-day trek from Takijiri-oji to Hongu. This covers 38.5km, with some ups and downs, and includes overnighting midway in either Takahara or Chikatsu-yu (or both). For a short taste, consider the last 7.5km to Hongu (starting at Hosshinmon-oji),

🚶 Kumano Culture

Starting around the 9th century, the wilds of the Kii Peninsula incubated a syncretic belief system, called **Shugendo**, that combined an early form of Shinto and Esoteric Buddhism with elements of folk religion, Taoism and shamanism.

In Shinto, *kami* (gods) are located in (among other things) impressive natural phenomena, such as mountains and waterfalls – of which Kii has many.

In Shugendo, these *kami* are also believed to be *gongen*, manifestations of the Buddha or bodhisattva. The practice of Shugendo includes acts of physical endurance, like hiking through the mountains, which is how the Kumano trails came to be.

Left Nakahechi Trail.
Below River cruise, Kumano-gawa.

which takes two to three hours, is mostly downhill and passes through farmland and forest. Hongu is the trail's biggest hub, where Kumano Hongu Taisha is located. In Hongu, a short (2km) but steep trail, called **Dainichi-goe**, runs to the hot-spring settlement Yunomine Onsen – perfect for a post-hike soak. Buses also make the short trip between Hongu and Yunomine Onsen.

Ridgeline views or a river cruise From Hongu, there are a couple of options: continuing on the two-day hike (26.8km) to Kumano Naichi Taisha, with an overnight stay in Koguchi. This part of the trail is considered more challenging, and includes a steep section in the middle, but the pay off is some fantastic **ridgeline views**. Or you can do as many pilgrims of old did: take a 90-minute **river cruise** on a sampan down the Kumano-gawa, which finishes right near Kumano Hayatama Taisha (p162) in Shingu. You'll need to take a bus form Hongu to the pier; book through **Kumano Travel** and request an English-speaking guide.

LEFT: BEIBAOKE/SHUTTERSTOCK ©
RIGHT: GONZALO AZUMENDI/ALAMY STOCK PHOTO ©

28

Temples by Day
& NIGHT

TEMPLES | CULTURE | HISTORY

Koya-san is a mountain monastery founded in the 9th century and still active today. It is a site of religious pilgrimage but also a popular tourist destination. The highlight for most visitors is Oku-no-in, a vast cemetery filled with moss-covered stone stupas set among towering cedars.

🗺 How to

When to go Koya-san's temples stay open year round but much of the town shuts down between December and February. Note that it is typically 7°C colder here than in Osaka or Kyoto.

Getting around You must take the bus from the cable car station into town (10 minutes; walking on the road is prohibited); the same bus travels to major sights and lodgings. The town is only 3km west to east (and 2km north to south), which means it's easy to get around on foot.

Koya-san In Buddhist iconography, Koya-san's setting amongst eight peaks resembles a lotus flower, with the peaks forming the petals. It is divided into two main areas: the **Garan** (Sacred Precinct) in the west and Oku-no-in in the east.

The Garan This is the monastery's teaching centre, which is still used today – you might see saffron-robed novices on the premises. While historically and culturally important, the Garan can be underwhelming to visitors, since almost all of the buildings are modern reconstructions (the originals having burned down numerous times throughout history). The most interesting structure is the **Konpon Daito**, a 48.5m-tall, bright-vermilion pagoda, located at what is considered to be the centre of the lotus-flower formed by Koya-san's eight mountains.

🏯 Temple Tours

For more insight into Koya-san's culture and history, book one of Awesome Tours' excellent tours or courses (awesome-tours.jp), led by English-speaking monks. The Oku-no-in night tour is highly recommended, as is the meditation and tea ceremony experience.

Above left Oku-no-in.
Above right Konpon Daito.
Left Garan.

Exploring Oku-no-in Oku-no-in means 'inner sanctuary', and it is one of the most spiritual places in Japan. At its furthest reaches is the crypt of Koya-san's founder, Kobo Daishi. Spread out before it are some 200,000 tombs, creating Japan's largest cemetery. These were built during various historical eras by people, prominent and otherwise, who wanted their remains (or at least a lock of hair) interred close to the legendary monk. Enter Oku-no-in at Ichi-no-hashi, from where it is 2km to Gobyo. On return, you can take a shorter walk down, along the Naka-no-hashi route to the Oku-no-in-mae bus stop, where you can catch a bus back to town (or walk it in about 30 minutes). Oku-no-in is very photogenic – on early misty mornings, when the afternoon sun beams through the trees, and in winter under a blanket of snow. It's OK to take

🏯 Kobo Daishi

Kobo Daishi (774–835; also known as Kukai) is one of the most prominent figures in Japanese cultural history, influential in the spread of Buddhism in Japan and credited with founding many temples.

In the early 9th century, he travelled to China to study esoteric Buddhism and later established Koya-san as a place for worship and study.

In 835, as his health was in decline, he begin fasting and meditating. He entered a crypt that he asked to be sealed upon his death, never to be opened again. His followers carried out his wishes, but to this day there are some who believe Kobo Daishi is still alive, meditating for eternity.

Left Kobo Daishi.
Below Toro-do.

photographs up to the bridge, Gobyo-bashi. To the right of Gobyo-bashi are bronze effigies of the bodhisattva Jizo that visitors ladle water over as a way of praying for the souls of the departed.

Miroku-ishi and Toro-do Just beyond the bridge is a wooden building the size of a large phone booth, which contains the Miroku-ishi, a stone said to weigh as much as your sins. Reach through the hole and try to lift it onto the shelf. (Don't feel bad if your sins are too much to handle: most people can't manage the feat.) Next is the Toro-do, a large hall full of lanterns. Two of the large ones in the back of the hall are said to have been lit uninterruptedly for more than 900 years. Other lanterns have been donated by dignitaries, including emperors and prime ministers.

Gobyo Behind the Toro-do is the wooden, thatched-roof gate that marks the entry to Gobyo, Kobo Daishi's crypt. This is as far as anyone can go. For many, a visit here is an act of pilgrimage. People chant sutras and light incense and candles. You don't need to be a believer to join the procession – just be respectful.

LEFT: MIRKO KUZMANOVIC/SHUTTERSTOCK ©
RIGHT: MATHIAS RHODE/ALAMY STOCK PHOTO ©

Staying in a Temple Lodge

SEE A BUDDHIST TEMPLE FROM THE INSIDE OUT

To stay in a *shukubo*, a lodging at a Buddhist temple, is to go beyond sightseeing and engage more deeply with Japanese culture. There are opportunities to join morning rites and to sample *shojin-ryori* (Buddhist vegetarian cuisine).

Left *Shukubo*, Koya-san.
Centre *Shojin-ryori* at a *shukubo*.
Right Slippers at a *shukubo*.

JOHN LANDER/ALAMY STOCK PHOTO ©

Historically, *shukubo* were created for pilgrims who, as early as the Heian period (794–1185), set off on foot, usually from Kyoto, to worship or perform austerities at temples in the mountains. Indeed some *shukubo* are still used solely for this purpose (though many pilgrims now arrive via bus); however, there are also many temples that have opened their lodgings to the general public. Reservations are a must.

Choosing a Temple

S*hukubo* vary greatly and can be found all over Japan. Some are humble, with shared facilities and sliding screens to partition rooms. Others may have en-suite baths, lifts and garden views. Sleeping is typically on futons (quilt-like mattresses) laid out on tatami-mat floors, though there are some temples that offer Western-style beds. Most allow visitors to observe the monks' morning prayer rituals. Some also offer meditation experiences.

Mountain monastery Koya-san (p156) is the most popular place to experience a *shukubo*. There are over 50 here and some are especially accommodating towards overseas guests, with English-speakers who can explain some of the monks' practices and beliefs.

Prices are fixed: the most basic rooms start at ¥9900 per person for one night and two meals, based on double occupancy. Most temples charge a surcharge for solo travellers. The **Koyasan Shukubo Association** (eng-shukubo.net) can assist with making reservations.

The Ins & Outs of Staying in a Shukubo

Temples typically follow strict timelines and guests are expected to follow them. Check-in is expected by 5pm at the latest, and many temples want you to inform them in advance if you won't arrive on time. Few will hold dinner, which typically happens at 6pm.

Morning prayers typically start around 6am. Breakfast is often served just after, around 7am. You can skip morning prayers and roll up to breakfast late, but it will likely be cold.

> *Shukubo* vary greatly and can be found all over Japan.

Like other Japanese-style lodgings, you should take your shoes off at the entrance, swapping them for slippers. The slippers are for use in the corridors and are not to be worn on *tatami* (socks are OK). In your room, there will be a *yukata* (light cotton kimono) or pyjamas to wear around the temple.

Shojin-ryori

Shukubo serve authentic *shojin-ryori* – Japan's Buddhist cuisine, which contains no meat, fish or any animal product or pungent aromatics (like garlic) – at dinner and breakfast. A typical meal includes tofu prepared a few different ways; seasonal vegetables served steamed, as tempura or pickled; a soup made with a kelp-based broth; and rice. Many temples also serve lunch to non-staying guests (reservations required) – so you don't absolutely have to stay in a *shukubo* to experience *shojin-ryori*.

🏯 Best Temple Stays

Eko-in (ekoin.jp) The best all-around temple, managed by a team of English-speaking monks. In Koya-san.

Shojoshin-in (shojoshinin.jp) Atmospheric temple with a thatched roof and humble (but comfortable) rooms. In Koya-san.

Ichijo-in (itijyoin.or.jp) Koya-san temple, known for its beautifully presented, gourmet *shojin-ryori*.

Shunko-in (shunkoin.com) Excellent place for a *shukubo* experience in Kyoto. The head priest speaks English, and you can try Zen meditation.

Saikan Atop Mt Haguro, one of the three sacred peaks that make up Yamagata's Dewa Sanzan, historically a place of pilgrimage for mountain ascetics.

Listings

BEST OF THE REST

🏯 Shrines & Temples

Kumano Hongu Taisha

Of the three grand shrines of Kumano, this one is noteworthy for its traditional architecture: note the criss-crossing roof beams and the elegant, unvarnished wood. In Hongu; arrive on foot or by bus from Kii-Tanabe.

Kumano Nachi Taisha

Shrine built on the side of a mountain as a place to worship the spectacular Nachi-no-taki, Japan's tallest waterfall. Near Kii-Katsuura; get here by bus, or on foot.

Kumano Hayatama Taisha

Ancient shrine (whose building is a modern reconstruction) with a sacred *nagi* (Asian bayberry tree) believed to be 800 years old. Walk or take the bus from Shingu Station, or arrive via sampan.

Otorii

The largest *torii* (Shinto shrine gate) in Japan – 33.9m tall and 42m wide, made out of steel and painted dramatic black – marks the entrance to Oyunohara, the sandbank that was the original site of Kumano Hongu Taisha.

Konpon Daito

The object of worship inside this Koya-san pagoda is Dainichi-nyorai (Cosmic Buddha), surrounded by four attendant Buddhas and, painted on pillars, 16 bodhisattva, which together compose a three-dimensional mandala.

Toko-ji

Like many hot-spring-adjacent temples, this small one in Yunomine is dedicated to Yakushi Nyorai, the medicine Buddha.

♨ Onsen

Tsubo-yu

Teeny tiny private hot spring – a wooden shack over a river – that holds two people max. Pay admission at the adjacent public bathhouse (which you can visit afterwards) and wait your turn. In Yunomine.

Kawa-yu

Visit Kii in winter (December to February) for Kawa-yu's 'Sennin-buro' – a section of the river bank that is dug out each season to create a large, naturally heated, public bathing pool. Near Yunomine; access is by bus from Hongu.

🏛 Museums & Cultural Centres

Kumano Hongu Heritage Centre

Contemporary multimedia complex in Hongu with exhibits about Kumano's culture and natural environment, plus English-speaking staff and resources for travellers.

Reihokan

Koya-san museum housing some of the important artworks belonging to the area's many temples.

THE ASAHI SHIMBUN VIA GETTY IMAGES ©

Reihokan.

TRIALIST/SHUTTERSTOCK ©

Guesthouses

J-Hoppers Kumano Yunomine ¥

An old *minshuku* turned hostel, with shared facilities – including three small onsen baths that can be used privately. In Yunomine, and popular with international travellers.

Blue Sky Guesthouse ¥¥

Fantastic guesthouse located in a quiet glen just outside central Hongu. All rooms have private facilities and the English-speaking owner is a great source of local information.

Tofu & Vegetarian

Bononsha ¥

Boho chill vegetarian cafe in Koya-san. Come after 11am for the excellent daily lunch plate, served until they run out. Good coffee and chai, too. English menu.

Hamadaya ¥¥

Famous Koya-san purveyor of *goma-dofu* (sesame tofu), made with mountain spring water and blessed with Buddhist chanting.

Hanabishi Honten ¥¥

Long-running Koya-san restaurant that serves classic, Koya-style *shojin ryori* (Buddhist vegetarian cuisine).

Cafe Bocu ¥¥

Macrobiotic lunch plates and fresh-baked bread. In Chikatsu-yu, a village along the Kumano Kodo. Open for lunch.

Kadohama ¥¥

Koya-san restaurant specialising in *goma-dofu*, with beautifully presented lunch sets in bamboo baskets. English menu.

Ichijo-in ¥¥¥

Koya-san temple, known for its beautifully plated, gourmet *shojin-ryori*, which has lunch service for non-staying guests. Reservations essential.

Kumano Hongu Taisha.

Coffee & Snacks

Komi Coffee ¥

Cosy coffee stop (with beans from a small roaster in Hokkaido) near the entrance to Oku-no-in in Koya-san. Curries, sandwiches and apple pie, too. English menu.

Choux ¥

Takeaway counter selling fresh-made cream puffs and coffee. In Hongu (near the Dainichi-goe trailhead).

Dinner & Drinks

Kumano.co Shokudo ¥¥

Small plates made with local ingredients, like river fish and venison, paired with craft beer and gin cocktails. In Hongu; open late.

Shinbe ¥¥

Local *izakaya* (Japanese pub-eatery) with excellent seafood. In Tanabe and popular with travellers setting out on the Kumano Kodo.

 Scan for more things to see, do and try on Kii Peninsula

HIROSHIMA & WESTERN HONSHU

CYCLING | SHRINE | MUSEUM

Experience Hiroshima & Western Honshu online

ITZAVU/SHUTTERSTOCK ©

HIROSHIMA & WESTERN HONSHU
Trip Builder

Apart from Hiroshima City, western Honshu doesn't receive many tourists, which is great for those seeking adventure off the beaten path. Sprawling ancient shrine compounds, an original castle, well-preserved Edo-era merchant districts, and unique gardens and museums are easy to explore at your own pace.

Tour the shrine where the Shinto gods meet annually, **Izumo Taisha** (p170)
🕐 1 day

Reflect on the tragic past of this cosmopolitan city at the **Hiroshima Peace Memorial Museum** (p180)
🕐 1 day

Eat oysters prepared as you like them on **Miyajima** (p171)
🕐 ½ day

Explore bookable experiences in Hiroshima & Western Honshu online

Sea of Japan

Sea of Hibiki

Sea of Aki

Sea of Suo

Sea of Iyo

Oda

Gotsu

Hamada

Tsuwano

Higashi-fukawa

Kogushi

Hatsukaichi

Miyajima

Hiroshim

Eta-jima

Kur

Iwakuni

Hofu

Tokuyama

Shimonoseki

Ube

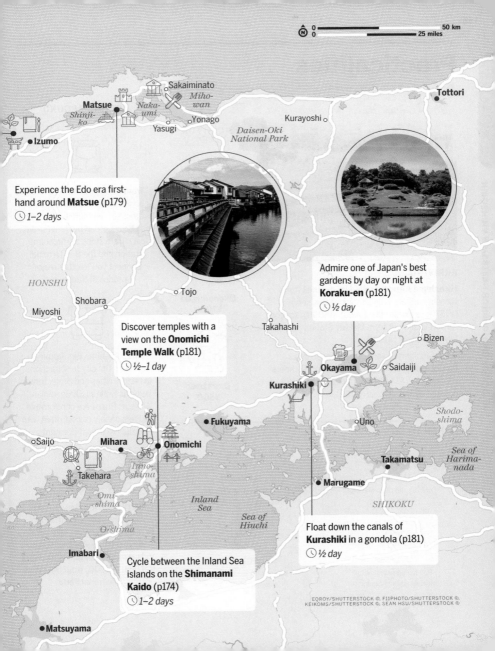

Tottori

Sakaiminato
Miho-wan
Yonago
Daisen-Oki National Park
Kurayoshi

Matsue
Shinji-ko
Naka-umi
Yasugi

Izumo

Experience the Edo era first-hand around **Matsue** (p179)
🕐 *1–2 days*

o Tojo

Admire one of Japan's best gardens by day or night at **Koraku-en** (p181)
🕐 *½ day*

HONSHU

Shobara

Miyoshi

Takahashi

o Bizen

Discover temples with a view on the **Onomichi Temple Walk** (p181)
🕐 *½–1 day*

o Saidaiji

Okayama

Kurashiki

o Saijo

Mihara
Teno-shima

Onomichi

● Fukuyama

o Uno

Shodo-shima

Takehara

Omi-shima

Inland Sea

Sea of Hiuchi

Sea of Harima-nada

Takamatsu

O-shima

● Marugame

SHIKOKU

Imabari

Float down the canals of **Kurashiki** in a gondola (p181)
🕐 *½ day*

Cycle between the Inland Sea islands on the **Shimanami Kaido** (p174)
🕐 *1–2 days*

● Matsuyama

EQROY/SHUTTERSTOCK ©, F11PHOTO/SHUTTERSTOCK ©,
KEIKOMS/SHUTTERSTOCK ©, SEAN HSU/SHUTTERSTOCK ©

Practicalities

DECOPLUS/SHUTTERSTOCK ©

ARRIVING

Hiroshima Airport Around 50 minutes from Hiroshima Station by Limousine Bus service (¥1370) or private taxi (about ¥17,000). Yonago Airport is an hour from Matsue Station by Limousine Bus (¥1000).

Train Shinkansen service from Tokyo takes four hours to Hiroshima (¥19,440) or 3½ hours to Okayama (¥17,700). Both destinations are covered by the JR Pass (p000).

HOW MUCH FOR

Two raw oysters
¥500

Okonomiyaki
¥1000

Draft beer
¥500

GETTING AROUND

Tram Hiroshima doesn't have an extensive subway system, but most of the tourist attractions can be accessed by tram (street car). Tram stops at Hiroshima Station and the Bus Terminal connect you to other major modes of transport.

Bus Hiroshima Bus Terminal connects the city to attractions in nearby cities and prefectures, such as Iwakuni, Onomichi and Matsue. Buses are comfortable and reasonably priced, often with valuable tourist discounts.

Ferry Service to Miyajima is available from Miyajima Pier (¥180), but you must take a train ride to the pier. Another scenic and convenient option is the Aqua Net boat (¥2200) from the Peace Memorial Park.

WHEN TO GO

JAN–MAR
Cold, dry and clear; fine with warm clothing

APR–JUN
Mild with occasional rain, increasingly rainy from June

JUL–SEP
Hot, humid and rainy, but improving by mid-September

OCT–DEC
Mild and dry weather, great for enjoying autumn foliage

TOP: MIKA /GETTY IMAGES ©
BOTTOM: OKMO/SHUTTERSTOCK ©

EATING & DRINKING

Iwakuni-zushi A local style of preserved sushi served like a slice of cake. Try it at one of several restaurants at either end of Kintai-kyo in Iwakuni.

Sea bream This is a versatile fish is caught in Japan's Inland Sea. The fishing port of Tomo-no-ura is famous for restaurants serving traditional sea-bream dishes.

Hiroshima-style ramen (chilled noodles dipped in a rich broth) Locals like their *tsukemen* broth spicy, with plenty of chilli oil. Start with the lowest level and turn up the heat to your liking!

Must-try
Lopez Okonomiyaki (p180)

Best foodie neighbourhood
Hiroshima's Hondori

CONNECT & FIND YOUR WAY

Wi-fi Japan Wi-Fi is a free service available nationwide. Download the app to connect automatically when you are near hotspots. For a faster connection with wider coverage, rent a pocket wi-fi from Japan Wireless (japan-wireless.com).

Navigation Navigation apps will help you to find locations and figure out how to get there, so wi-fi is critical.

VISIT HIROSHIMA TOURIST PASS

Buy the Visit Hiroshima Tourist Pass for one, two or three days for unlimited use of trams, many buses, and ferries to Miyajima, plus local business discounts.

WHERE TO STAY

Many choose Hiroshima as a base, but reasonable midrange hotels are available throughout western Honshu so you can city-hop without breaking your budget.

Place	Pro/Con
Hiroshima	Large number of midrange hotels downtown and around Hiroshima Station.
Okayama	Plenty of budget and midrange hotels south and east of Okayama Station.
Matsue	Western-style hotels and ryokan around Matsue Station and north of Ohashi-gawa.
Yanago	Mainly budget hotels around Yanago Station and reasonable Japanese-style hotels near Kaike Onsen.
Shimanami Kaido	Countless hotels, guesthouses and hostels in every town along the route. Larger rooms allow bicycle storage.

MONEY

Cash is king, but invest in a PASPY transit card to make it easier to ride trains and buses. Breaking ¥10,000 bills at convenience stores is not a problem, even for small items.

29 Shrines & TEMPLES

ARCHITECTURE | FESTIVALS | RELIGION

Everyone knows Miyajima's floating *torii* (shrine gate) on the Inland Sea, but western Honshu is home to other famous and older places of worship. Explore Daisen, the mountain home of the mystical Shugendo religion; Kibitsu-jinja, which inspired the Japanese legend of Momotaro; and other places of spiritual significance.

How to

When to go Spring and autumn for beautiful foliage. Avoid the crowded holiday period the first few days of the year.

Annual festivals Rei Tai-sai Matsuri (14 May) at Izumo Taisha has archery rituals. Kangen-sai is a popular August music and dance festival on Miyajima. A 2000-torch parade marks the start of the Daisen Summer Festival in June.

Shrine and temple etiquette Be respectful of worshippers and keep your voice low.

Izumo Taisha Japan's second most important shrine, after Ise-jingu, is where Shinto gods are said to gather once a year to discuss the affairs of humankind. Its founding pre-dates written history, but it's rebuilt using traditional methods every 60 to 70 years. The sprawling grounds and huge wooden buildings are impressive, especially if you stand beneath the *shimenawa* (sacred rope) at the entry of the worship hall.

Daisen This majestic mountain overlooking western Tottori was once sacred for thousands of warrior monks who practiced Shugendo,

Above right Izumo Taisha.
Below right Daisen-ji.

TANG YAN SONG/SHUTTERSTOCK ©

🏛 Japanese Religions

Shinto is considered the indigenous religion but when Buddhism came to Japan in the 7th century the two intermingled, which is often seen in their art and architecture. Folk religions joined the mix creating Shugendo, often practiced in the mountains and requiring strict physical training.

a melding of Buddhism, Shinto and shamanism. It's home to **Daisen-ji**, built in the 8th century and today an important temple of the Tendai Buddhist sect where visitors can practice *zazen* (seated meditation) or walk in the lush forests.

Miyajima Best known for its floating *torii* of **Itsukushima-jinja** on the calm waters of the Inland Sea, Miyajima means 'Shrine Island', with many other small shrines around Misen. Hike or take the ropeway up to the summit of **Misen** for a spectacular view of Hiroshima Bay.

Kibitsu-jinja and Kibitsuhiko-jinja These two shrines in Okayama are related to the legendary hero **Momotaro** (aka 'peach boy') and can be visited together via a pleasant 17km cycling path along the Kibi plain.

TANYA JONES/SHUTTERSTOCK ©

Shrine, Temple
OR BOTH?

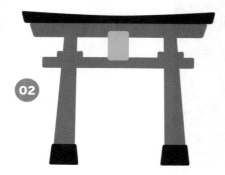

01 Goshuin
Unique stamps available for a small fee at many (not all) temples and shrines, collected in a book called *goshuincho*.

02 Torii
The traditional gate of a Shinto shrine, marking the boundary between the ordinary world and the sacred.

03 Chozuya
A trough of water used to purify your hands and mouth before entering a shrine.

04 Shimenawa
A woven rope of straw or hemp used in Shinto to denote a place or object that is sacred.

05 Komainu
A pair of statues in the shape of lion-dogs that guard shrines from evil.

06 Ema
Originating from Shinto but now used by Buddhist temples too; wooden plaques on which visitors can write their prayers and wishes.

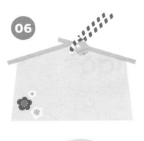

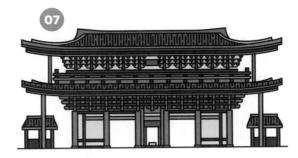

07 Sanmon

The largest and most important gate of a Buddhist temple. It is usually located between the *sonmon* (outer gate) and the main hall.

08 Bonsho

A large bronze bell used in ceremonies at a temple; it is rung 108 times for the New Year.

09 Nio

A pair of fierce-looking guardian carvings or statues which protect Buddhist temples from evil.

10 Jizo

This jovial-appearing Buddhist statue represents a god who protects children and travellers and is a favourite deity in Japanese culture.

11 Omamori

These small charms can be purchased from shrines to protect you from various misfortunes or grant you luck in specific situations.

01 LO KIN-HEI/SHUTTERSTOCK ©, 02 SENRYU/GETTY IMAGES ©, 03 YUKIK/SHUTTERSTOCK ©, 04 SENRYU/GETTY IMAGES ©, 05 MIRJANA UZELAC/SHUTTERSTOCK ©, 06 T-K-M/SHUTTERSTOCK © 07 VECTOR TRADITION/SHUTTERSTOCK ©, 08 KISASAGE/SHUTTERSTOCK ©, 09 TERA.KEN/SHUTTERSTOCK ©, 10 SIMPLY AMAZING/ SHUTTERSTOCK ©, 11 KASAMARAT/SHUTTERSTOCK ©

30 CYCLING THE
Shimanami Kaido

CYCLING | SIGHTSEEING | SEA

The Shimanami Kaido is a 70km cycling path hopping various islands between Honshu and Shikoku. It is one of Japan's best two-wheel road trips, easily customisable in length and difficulty, with breathtaking scenery around every curve.

KURUTANX/SHUTTERSTOCK ©

🗺 Trip Notes

Where to start Onomichi, a seaport town halfway between Hiroshima and Okayama.

When to go You can cycle year-round; greater likelihood of heavy rain or typhoons from mid-June to mid-September.

Take your time The route can be cycled in a day, but you'll enjoy it more if you allow at least two days.

How much Bicycles can be rented from ¥2000 per day, plus a ¥1100 deposit.

🚲 100% Cycle-Friendly

The Shimanami Kaido was made for cyclists from all over the world, with luggage forwarding and storage services, bike-friendly transport and accommodation, and plenty of English signage. When in doubt, follow the blue line painted on the road with directions and mileage to each end point.

HONSHU

Mihara •

Onomichi •

Mukai-shima

01 On Ikuchi-jima, **Kosan-ji** is a wealthy businessman's gaudy tribute to his mother, with over-the-top replicas of art from other temples. Love it or hate it, Choseikaku Villa is a masterpiece.

Takehara •

02 The 1400-year-old shrine of **Oyamazumi-jinja** on Omi-shima is home to a collection of Japan's most important samurai artefacts among a cluster of camphor trees up to 2600 years old.

Inno-shima

Ikuchi-jima

Omi-shima

Hakata-jima

04 The sight and aroma of thousands of rose bushes in bloom from May to November make **Yoshiumi Rose Park** a good rest stop on Oshima, especially for some rose-flavoured ice cream.

O-shima

03 Run by a fishing cooperative, **Noshima Ferry Terminal Restaurant** sells the freshest seafood around Oshima. Throw some on the BBQ for a quick recharge on your ride.

05 The 307-m high **Kirosan Observatory** on Oshima is considered the finest viewpoint along the Shimanami Kaido. Arrive at the golden hour for a memorable sunset.

Inland Sea

Imabari •

SHIKOKU

TETSU SNOWDROP/SHUTTERSTOCK ©
BLACKRABBIT3/SHUTTERSTOCK ©

31 Hiroshima's
SOUL FOOD

GRILL | DINING | LOCAL

According to locals, *okonomiyaki* in any other city is just a snack. In Hiroshima, it's a meal, and one to be enjoyed around a communal grill with both friends and strangers. There is no doubt that this savoury dish – part crêpe, part pancake, part noodle, part toppings – is Hiroshima's soul food, and one you must try if you visit the city.

JUNICHI MIYAZAKI/LONELY PLANET ©

How to

Where to find it Look for お好み焼き on signs or visit one of the two major centres: Okonomimura in Hatchibori or Okonomi Monogatari Ekimae Hiroba across from Hiroshima Station.

How to order *Okonomiyaki* means 'grilled as you like it', so feel free to customise. Most shops have picture menus to point and select.

Vegetarian or vegan? *Okonomiyaki* can be meatless, but there will always be some lard, a consideration if you're vegan or eat halal or kosher.

History *Okonomiyaki* got its current form post-WWII, when food was scarce in Hiroshima but large sheets of metal to turn into grills were not. It was based on a snack called *issen yoshoku* (known as 'Western food' earlier), but more substantial ingredients such as eggs, seafood and noodles were added to make it a true meal. Many older residents fondly remember the days of *okonomiyaki* street stalls filling the air with their fragrance, and the dish remains Hiroshima's favourite local food nearly 80 years later.

Above *Okonomiyaki.*
Above right Restaurant in Okonomimura.
Below right *Okonomiyaki.*

LUCAS VALLECILLOS/ALAMY STOCK PHOTO ©

No DIY? Customers can't cook their own Hiroshima-style *okonomiyaki* (unlike the Osaka-style dish). Master Fernando Lopez of Lopez Okonomiyaki (p180) explains that the various layers involved have to be cooked separately, taking up too much real estate on the grill for individual customers to make their own.

The fun of dining Part of the fun of eating *okonomiyaki* in Hiroshima is the communal dining experience. Guests sit around the grill and the master and assistants work behind it. Not only is it fun to watch, but it's easy to engage in conversation with chef and customers alike. Try using a mix of English, Japanese and hand gestures, and you might end up with a newfound friendship. The stalls of Okonomimura have a good mix of tourists and locals.

> ### ⚡ Eat Okonomiyaki Like a Local
>
> Locals eat *okonomiyaki* right off the grill, but remember it's still cooking while you're eating, so the flavour is changing. If you eat too slowly, it can overcook, so pay attention to the speed.
>
> ---
>
> **Tips by Fernando Lopez**
> *Okonomiyaki Master,*
> *Okonomiyaki Lopez*
> *@okonomiyakilopez*

ARTTRAN/GETTY IMAGES ©

32 Western Honshu
DAY TRIPS

CASTLE | HISTORY | MUSEUM

▬▬▬ Beyond the requisite Peace Memorial Park, Peace Memorial Museum and the island of Miyajima, the Hiroshima area has plenty to offer if you're willing to hop on a bus and explore for a day. Edo-period castles, centuries-old sake breweries and even museums of the supernatural are all interesting side trips from Hiroshima city.

MILOSZ MASLANKA/SHUTTERSTOCK ©

📸 How to

Sightseeing buses Bus tours run by JR Chugoku (chugoku-jrbus.co.jp) are organised to many destinations around Hiroshima city suitable for day trips. Most of these depart from Hiroshima Station to areas like Iwakuni and Takehara.

Discounts for foreign tourists Promotions have been changing, but discounted rates on sightseeing buses for foreign-passport holders seem to be constant around Hiroshima; be sure to ask.

LIANG YU/SHUTTERSTOCK ©

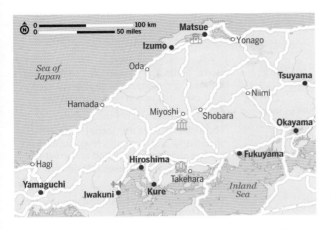

Above left Kintai-kyo.
Below left Takehara.

Iwakuni The five-arched bridge – **Kintai-kyo** – in Iwakuni is one of Japan's architectural wonders. It's particularly beautiful in spring, framed by pink cherry blossoms. You'll also get a great view of the bridge and the city beyond it from **Iwakuni-jo**, the castle located on a hillside 200m above the river.

Miyoshi In the mountains north of Hiroshima, Miyoshi hosts the recently built **Mononoke Museum**, dedicated to the spirit demons of Japanese culture, known as *mononoke* or *yokai* (p90). There's a huge rotating collection of art and historical items relating to the supernatural world, augmented by engaging interactive content created by the multimedia company teamLab. The location was chosen because of an infamous event that occurred in Miyoshi in the 18th century involving a young samurai who was visited by *yokai* for 30 consecutive nights; the story is documented in illustrations on a scroll which is on display in the museum.

Takehara This coastal city east of Hiroshima has a beautifully preserved historical district, notably populated with several sake breweries that have been operating for over 250 years. One of them is the family brewery of **Masataka Taketsuru**, known as the father of Japanese whisky. A small sake museum within the brewery is open on weekends. Nearby **Fujii Shuzo** brewery has sake tasting, or enjoy it paired with a simple meal of soba noodles at the on-site restaurant, **Tanizaki**.

Matsue-jo on the Cheap

A discounted bus ticket available from the Hiroshima Bus Centre enables foreign-passport holders to travel to Matsue in Shimane Prefecture for ¥500 (regular fare is ¥4000).

Though it's more overnight trip than a day trip, this discount enables you to visit picturesque Matsue-jo, one of only 12 original castles remaining in Japan.

The castle area contains Edo-period neighbourhoods and several interesting museums, as well as a moat and river infrastructure with sightseeing boat tours.

Listings

BEST OF THE REST

⫽ Locally Famous Cuisine

Tomoe-an ¥¥¥

A restaurant housed in a beautiful former ryokan with private dining rooms, near Matsue Station. Try the Shimane beef, a high-grade *wagyu* known for its lingering umami flavour and melt-in-your-mouth texture.

Shimada Fisheries Oyster Hut ¥¥

All the fresh, grilled Hiroshima oysters you can eat in an hour, about a 10-minute walk from Miyajima ferry terminal.

Ajidokoro Misa ¥¥¥

Sakaiminato, in Tottori Prefecture, provides western Japan with nearly its entire supply of crab, so the crab served here is as fresh as possible. Try it grilled, boiled or in *shabu-shabu* (beef or pork cooked with vegetables).

Heike Chaya ¥¥

The skilled chefs of Shimonoseki, in Yamaguchi Prefecture, are famed for their preparation of *fugu* (poisonous pufferfish), which can be eaten raw as sashimi or cooked in numerous ways. Superior views of the Kanmon Straits.

Lopez Okonomiyaki ¥

Master Fernando Lopez trained at Hiroshima's famous *okonomiyaki* shop Hassho over two decades ago, and is the man who accidentally added the now popular jalapeño pepper as a Hiroshima-style topping.

⚱ Unique Museums

Hiroshima Peace Memorial Museum

Hiroshima's premier museum located inside the Peace Memorial Park has a collection of items salvaged from the aftermath of the atomic bomb. The displays are confronting and personal, and some of the photographs are grim, but, while upsetting, it's a must-see.

Shoji Ueda Museum of Photography

The architecture of this Tottori museum showcasing one of Japan's favourite modern photographers was designed to highlight its commanding view of nearby Daisen.

Mizuki Shigeru Museum

This museum in Sakaiminato honours manga artist Mizuki Shigeru, creator of famous cartoons about the supernatural world of *yokai*. Mizuki Shigeru Rd between the museum and train station is lined with 177 bronze statues of characters created by Mizuki.

Betty Smith Jeans Museum

Learn how these high-quality Japanese jeans are made in Kurashiki (Okayama Prefecture), and even customise a pair of jeans for yourself as a unique souvenir.

Adachi Museum of Art

Besides the art on display inside this museum, located in Yasugi in Shimane Prefecture, the building's design frames the living art of the manicured Japanese gardens outside.

Kurashiki.

SEAN3810/GETTY IMAGES ©

☼ The Scenic Inland Sea

Tomo-no-ura

A picture-perfect historic fishing village of eastern Hiroshima Prefecture. The charming architecture is said to be the inspiration for the Studio Ghibli–animated film *Ponyo*.

Okunoshima

Also known as 'Rabbit Island', this tiny island is home to hundreds of cute feral rabbits. In odd juxtaposition, there's also a small Poison Gas Museum memorialising the Japanese Imperial Army's illegal production of chemical weapons during WWII.

Rabbits, Okunoshima.

Onomichi Temple Walk

The starting point of the Shimanami Kaido (p174) has a famous 'Temple Walk' connecting 25 of the city's temples on a path that winds through the backstreets, with scenic views from the hillside along the way.

Tobishima Kaido

An alternative to the popular Shimanami Kaido, this 30km cycling route starts on Shimo-kamagari and ends on Okamura-jima. There are few bike-rental and support services along the way, so plan your trip carefully.

Kurashiki

Take a peaceful gondola ride down the historic canals of this merchant city, with its preserved Edo-period Bikan quarter full of interesting shops, cafes and restaurants.

❀ Local Spirits

Miyoshi Winery

This winery in the mountains of Hiroshima offers free tasting of its standard line-up of wines, or taste a flight of its premium Tomoe line for a fee.

Doppo-kan   ¥¥

Formerly a sake brewery, Okayama's Doppo-kan added a line of German-inspired microbrewed beers in 1995 and began distilling whisky in 2011, followed by gin and vodka. Taste its products on-site or enjoy them with a meal in its restaurant, Shusei no Kagayaki.

✿ Beautiful Gardens

Koraku-en

One of Japan's best gardens, built to entertain feudal lords and officials visiting Okayama. It's beautifully illuminated on summer nights, when visitors can enjoy food and drink on the vast lawn like the nobles of yesteryear.

Sesshu Teien

Part of Yamaguchi's Joei-ji, this garden is a recognised National Site of Scenic Beauty. It was built as a stroll alking garden to be admired from many viewpoints, and can be enjoyed differently in all four seasons.

Yushien

A large Japanese-style garden on an island in Shimane Prefecture's brackish Lake Nakaumi. The jewels of the garden are its 250 species of peonies, which bloom in a hothouse year-round or in the garden itself mid-spring.

Scan to find more things to see, do and try in Hiroshima & Western Honshu online

AMY SHEEHAN/SHUTTERSTOCK ©

KYUSHU

ONSEN | SAMURAI | RURAL

Experience Kyushu online

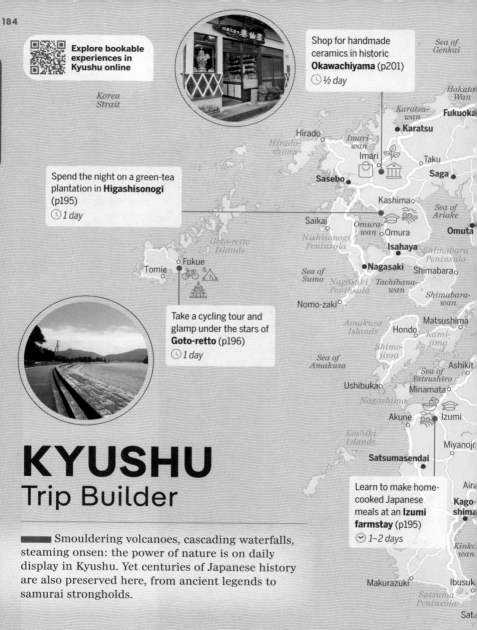

Explore bookable experiences in Kyushu online

Shop for handmade ceramics in historic **Okawachiyama** (p201)
🕐 ½ day

Spend the night on a green-tea plantation in **Higashisonogi** (p195)
🕐 1 day

Take a cycling tour and glamp under the stars of **Goto-retto** (p196)
🕐 1 day

Learn to make home-cooked Japanese meals at an **Izumi farmstay** (p195)
🕐 1–2 days

KYUSHU
Trip Builder

▬▬▬ Smouldering volcanoes, cascading waterfalls, steaming onsen: the power of nature is on daily display in Kyushu. Yet centuries of Japanese history are also preserved here, from ancient legends to samurai strongholds.

Korea Strait

Sea of Genkai

Hakata Wan

Karatsu-wan

Karatsu

Fukuoka

Hirado

Hirado-shima

Imari-wan

Imari

Taku

Sasebo

Kashima

Saga

Sea of Ariake

Saikai

Omura-wan

Omura

Omuta

Goto-retto Islands

Nishisonogi Peninsula

Isahaya

Shimabara Peninsula

Tomie

Fukue

Sea of Sumo

Nagasaki-Peninsula

Nagasaki

Shimabara

Tachibana-wan

Shimabara-wan

Nomo-zaki

Amakusa Islands

Hondo

Matsushima

Kami-jima

Shimo-jima

Ashikit

Sea of Amakusa

Sea of Yatsushiro

Ushibuka

Minamata

Nagashima

Akune

Izumi

Koshiki Islands

Miyanoj

Satsumasendai

Air

Kago-shima

Kinka-wan

Makurazuki

Ibusuk

Satsuma Peninsula

Sat

Take a hot sand bath at
Hyotan Onsen (p200)
🕐 ½ day

Walk through Oita's history
along the **Kyushu OLLE's
Okubungo Course** (p201)
🕐 1 day

Chase waterfalls on the
**Kokonoe Yume Suspension
Bridge** (p201)
🕐 ½ day

Onsen-hop between baths
before staying in a ryokan at
Kurokawa Onsen (p189)
🕐 1 day

Kanmon Straits
Shimonoseki
Kitakyushu
Koga
Iizuka
Yukuhashi
Sea of Suo
Nakatsu
Usa
Kunisaki Peninsula
Kunisaki
Imabari
Matsuyama
Ozu
Yawatahama
Sea of Iyo
Kitsuki
Kurume
Hita
Kusu
Yufuin
Beppu-wan
Beppu
Oita
Usuki
Saiki
Sukumo
Shimanto City
(Nakamura)
Tosa-Shimizu
Kuju-san
Oguni
Aso
Taketa
umamoto
Takamori
Taketa
Nobeoka
Hyuga
Yatsushiro
Hitoyoshi
Taragi
kuchi
Ebino
Miyazaki
Pacific Ocean
Miyakonojo
akurajima
Nichinan
Tarumizu
Kushima
Kanoya
Shibushi-wan
Sea of Hyuga
Nejime
Osumi Straits

AJISAI13/SHUTTERSTOCK ©, ICOSHA/SHUTTERSTOCK ©,
ROMIX IMAGE/SHUTTERSTOCK ©, BOHISTOCK/GETTY IMAGES ©

Ⓝ
0
0
100 km
50 miles

Practicalities

MAHATHIR MOHD YASIN/SHUTTERSTOCK ©

ARRIVING

Train Shinkansen (bullet train) service from Tokyo Station takes five hours to Hakata, Fukuoka (¥23,390) and 6½ hours to Kagoshima (¥31,060).

Air Fukuoka Airport is just a few minutes by train to Hakata Station and central Fukuoka (¥260). Kumamoto, Nagasaki, Kagoshima and Oita all have major airports that are fairly far from the city. Renting a car from the airport is advisable when exploring these parts of Kyushu.

HOW MUCH FOR A

Handmade tea cup
¥1500

Private onsen (1hr)
¥1800

Bowl of ramen
¥700

GETTING AROUND

Train The Kyushu shinkansen line connects Fukuoka, Kumamoto and Kagoshima with the rest of the nation. Other major cities can be reached by local train lines, but not always conveniently.

Bus Highway buses are a convenient way to travel between major cities and tourist destinations in Kyushu. Major cities and airports have bus terminals where you can purchase tickets.

Car By far the most convenient way around Kyushu, unless you plan to stay in the area of one or two major cities. Major highways are easy to drive on, but beware of shortcuts involving mountainous roads which can be narrower than expected.

WHEN TO GO

JAN–MAR
Crisp, clear and sometimes windy; bundle up warmly

APR–JUN
Mild with sporadic rain, a lot in June; more rain in Southern Kyushu

JUL–SEP
Oppressively hot and humid, improving a bit in September

OCT–DEC
Milder temperatures and less rain; Kyushu's best season

TOP: PANU_OASIS/SHUTTERSTOCK ©
BOTTOM: YAN YIAMPAYA/SHUTTERSTOCK ©

EATING & DRINKING

Yatai The quintessential Kyushu dining experience are the *yatai* (hawker stalls) of Fukuoka, open from 6pm every evening. Ramen, *yakitori* (skewers) and fried *gyoza* (dumplings) are common, but each stall is unique and some serve dishes you won't find elsewhere. The key is not to fill up too quickly and keep moving to sample different dishes. *Yatai* dining is both a social and gastronomic experience – guests are encouraged to introduce themselves and engage in conversation, so make new friends over great food.

Must-try ramen	Best for first-timers
Hakata-style ramen	Mamichan (p201)

CONNECT & FIND YOUR WAY

Wi-fi Japan Wi-Fi is a free service available nationwide. Download the app to connect you automatically when you are near hotspots. For a faster connection with wider coverage, rent a pocket wi-fi from Japan Wireless (japanwireless.com).

Navigation Wi-fi is crucial as you'll need navigation apps to find locations and figure out how to get there.

WHERE TO STAY

You can stay in hotels anywhere, so pamper yourself at a Japanese ryokan. On a smaller budget, enjoy friendship and home-cooked meals at a farmstay, or retreat in nature by glamping.

Place	Pro/Con
Fukuoka	Plenty of hotels and hostels around Hakata Station and Fukuoka Airport; easy access to many local attractions.
Goto	Unique glamping sites and other affordable accommodation, but Goto is too remote to be a Kyushu base.
Yufuin	Many midrange to top-end ryokan options, but it can be crowded and pricey during high season.
Beppu	Ryokan and hotels in every price range exist here in onsen heaven; difficult access to the rest of Kyushu without a car.

DRIVING

If you plan to drive, bring an International Driving Permit (IDP) or for certain countries without an IDP, an official Japanese translation of your driver's license.

MONEY

Carry lots of cash; in some rural areas even finding an ATM can be an adventure. International withdrawals are easiest from the ATMs of JP Bank (at post offices) and 7-Eleven Bank (in 7-Eleven stores).

33 Hidden Onsen of KYUSHU

HOT SPRINGS | RELAXATION | CULTURE

Bubbling just below the surface of Kyushu are a multitude of different sources of geothermically heated mineral waters, the force behind thousands of onsen (hot spring) facilities ranging from public and private bathhouses to luxurious ryokan (inns). With so many choices to enjoy a relaxing soak, we narrow down the competition for the best of Kyushu's hidden onsen.

TOYOKAZU Y/SHUTTERSTOCK ©

🗺 How to

Getting around Choose an area with plenty of onsen in walking distance – Kurokawa, Yufuin or Ureshino – or rent a car if you want to visit different areas.

Onsen passes Some locations offer passes known as *nyuto tegata* to allow visitors to hop from one onsen to the next. Kurokawa Onsen pass allows visitors to enjoy any three onsen for just ¥1300.

BYOT Save money by bringing your own towel, otherwise you'll have to rent or buy one at each onsen.

TOP PHOTO CORPORATION/ALAMY STOCK PHOTO ©

Above left Kurokawa Onsen.
Below left Ureshino Onsen.

Kurokawa Onsen A collection of 29 onsen including public bathhouses and ryokan. The community takes great care to maintain a traditional feel for both facilities and the entire village. It's nestled in a valley, so you'll enjoy views of the forest and the sound of the river as you bathe. Kurokawa is beautiful at night, especially between January and March when it's illuminated with bamboo-carved ornaments.

Yunohira Onsen A mere 20-minute drive from the more famous Yufuin, Yunohira Onsen maintains a peaceful atmosphere on a single cobblestone street that seems unchanged in half a century. Visit Yunohira to relax in one or more of its 21 inns with their own onsen, without the crowds. For a budget onsen day trip, there are five public baths, each costing a mere ¥200 to use.

Ureshino Onsen Ureshino is accessible from the major cities of Fukuoka and Nagasaki by bus (not train), although it's worth the effort to get there. Enjoy strolling the streets of this quaint town with its tea shops and foot baths. More than 30 places to stay are clustered around the banks of Shiota-gawa, and most private facilities allow bathing by non-staying guests for a reasonable fee.

Waita Onsen This collection of onsen and ryokan is clustered around Waita-san, a mountain on the border between Kumamoto and Oita prefectures. Several facilities in the area offer coin-operated private baths for hourly usage with superb views and soothing waters.

♨ The Many Types of Onsen

Onsen are a well-regulated industry in Japan, with specific standards to ensure quality and safety.

There are 10 different water qualities that are defined, each with certain health benefits.

What types of water should you try? Simple alkaline springs are popular as beauty treatments, leaving your skin feeling smooth to the touch. Chloride springs are salty and said to be good for improving circulation and dry skin conditions. Acidic springs are common in Japan and purportedly good for treating dermatitis and psoriasis.

Give each one a try and stick with the ones that feel the best!

Onsen – Medicine & Relaxation

HISTORY AND ETIQUETTE OF JAPAN'S BATHING CULTURE

Natural hot springs are not unique to Japan, but nobody in the world loves the soothing mineral waters quite like the Japanese. How did onsen become such an important part of Japanese culture as a whole?

Left Plastic bath chairs for washing.
Centre Small towel folded on man's head during onsen soak.
Right Drying after leaving an onsen.

KUREMO/SHUTTERSTOCK ©

The Onsen Culture of Japan

According to legend, onsen – as hot springs are called in Japanese – have been a part of Japanese culture and history possibly as far back as 3000 years ago. They can reliably be traced to the 8th century, when they were mentioned in Japan's oldest text, the Man'yōshū. Whatever the case, enjoying a soak in the mineral-enriched waters of more than 25,000 onsen in Japan has been engrained in the local way of life for a long time.

The indigenous religion of Shinto places a high importance on cleanliness, so daily bathing has always been an important part of Japanese lifestyle. Before people understood how the various minerals found in hot-springs water interact with the human body, onsen were believed to have mystical healing powers and were sought out and prized by many, including prominent Buddhist monks. Long before onsen became popular with the masses, people would make lengthy pilgrimages to various hot springs based on ailments they were suffering from. Even the shogun recognised the healing properties of onsen and would send a magistrate to bring barrels of water daily from a chosen hot spring along the Tokaido Road between Kyoto and Edo (present-day Tokyo).

It wasn't until the mid-19th century that onsen made the shift from health spas to entertainment. With the advent of printing, several woodblock artists popularised onsen with prints and illustrated books of beautiful people enjoying the soothing waters and luxurious locations, and suddenly, everyone wanted to visit onsen not to cure their ailments but for fun and relaxation. Such is the attitude

that continues today, with onsen-hopping one of the favourite leisure activities for domestic tourists. They are even popular as company-sponsored trips, because socialising in onsen is seen as a way to build camaraderie among co-workers.

A Guide to Onsen Etiquette

Onsen are for relaxation, so familiarise yourself with this basic etiquette so you can spend more time relaxing and less time worrying.

The indigenous religion of Shinto places a high importance on cleanliness, so daily bathing has always been an important part of Japanese lifestyle.

Wash thoroughly Onsen are not for cleaning yourself, so make sure you scrub head to toe and rinse off any soap in the shower area before entering the mineral bath itself.

No clothes or towels No clothing of any kind is allowed in the bathwater, and if you're carrying the small towel from the shower area to cover yourself while walking around, leave it outside the bath or fold it up and rest it on top of your head.

Tattoos Generally, tattoos are forbidden in most public onsen facilities, though individual onsen may allow them. Often, small tattoos are permitted to be covered with a bandage. If you have large tattoos, your best bet is to rent a private onsen bath, which costs an average of ¥1500 to ¥2500 per hour.

Just chill The atmosphere of an onsen is peaceful, so remain silent or talk quietly – and definitely no splashing, swimming or misbehaviour in the bath.

♨ Tips from an onsen sommelier

Use your towel to regulate your body temperature. In the winter, a hot towel on your head can keep your body warm, especially when using an outdoor onsen. In the summer, a cool towel on your head can keep you from overheating too quickly.

Unless you have sensitive skin, it's not necessary to rinse off after using an onsen. Leaving the onsen water on your skin enables you to absorb more of the nutrients in the water.

Pat yourself dry to remove the liquid after bathing.

Tips from Tomoko Matsuo
Certified Onsen Sommelier, Shiga Prefecture

34 In the Steps of **SAMURAI**

SAMURAI | TRADITION | CASTLE

Kyushu's samurai history runs long and deep as a launching point for foreign invasions and sites of epic battles for power. Learn more about the legendary warriors of Japan's feudal history by visiting modern locations where ancient culture and architecture are well preserved.

How to

Getting around Samurai history is scattered throughout Kyushu, so travelling by car is the best way to visit various locations.

Not just castles You'll find samurai history near the castles, in the quarters which often contain well-maintained former samurai residences.

Samurai culture The life of samurai wasn't all about war; in times of peace, they also practiced Japanese arts such as *sado* (tea ceremony), *shodo* (calligraphy) and *ikebana* (flower arranging).

Shimabara-jo The last great battle of the Edo period, the **Shimabara Rebellion** saw mostly Christian peasants face off against the shogunate soldiers when a cruel lord raised taxes to fund this castle's construction while suppressing the region's Christians. While the current keep is a 1964 reconstruction, the inner bailey surrounded by a wide moat retains the formidable appearance of the fortress. Nearby in a samurai quarter, Shitanocho street has preserved examples of samurai residences that are free to tour.

Above right Shimabara-jo.
Below right Samurai residence, Kitsuki.

SEAN PAVONE/SHUTTERSTOCK ©

JOYMSHAJ40/SHUTTERSTOCK ©

⛫ Explore Castle Ruins

Only ruins of Oka-jo remain, but a stroll of the grounds of this former castle in Taketa, Oita Prefecture, will give you an idea of its once massive scale. Oka-jo was the site of many great samurai battles between warring Kyushu clans.

Kitsuki A lovely example of an Edo-period samurai town, with a pair of well-preserved districts flanking the old commercial area, a sight that is best admired from the slope of **Shioya-no-saka**. Several samurai residences are open to the public. It's a favourite location for visitors to dress in rented kimonos and stroll through the streets, snacking and shopping.

Swordsmith Matsunaga The master craftsman **Matsunaga** has been making swords for over 40 years in Arao, Kumamoto Prefecture. A visit to his workshop gives you a chance to see the swordmaking process up close and perhaps try your hand at forging red-hot steel. If you're lucky, Matsunaga might demonstrate his sword's quality by slicing through a rolled-up bamboo mat. Make reservations in advance by phone.

35 The Rural Charm of **FARMSTAYS**

HOMESTAY | RURAL | CULTURE

Seeing Japan through the eyes of a tourist is one experience; seeing Japan through the eyes of a local is completely different. Farmstay opportunities provide a glimpse into the everyday rural life of Japanese people and a chance to make lasting friendships.

KUMATO/SHUTTERSTOCK ©

🗺 **How to**

Take the plunge
While farmstays can produce communication challenges or social faux pas, don't be afraid to make some mistakes – Japanese people are gracious and forgiving.

Booking Regional tourism organisations and NPOs work with local families and can assign you to those most suitable for your situation.

Building bridges To ease any language barriers, sharing a set of photos of your country, city and daily life can help facilitate conversation with your hosts.

JOHN STEELE/ALAMY STOCK PHOTO ©

Above left Higashisonogi tea plantation.
Below left Rokugo Manzan.

Izumi This quiet coastal town in Kagoshima Prefecture is best known as the migration destination for thousands of Siberian cranes every winter. Farmstay hosts often love to show off their town, where visitors can stroll through a preserved district of samurai residences, dress in kimonos and experience a Japanese tea ceremony. Izumi City Tourism (izumi-navi.jp) coordinates farmstay experiences for about 18 households, some of whom are fluent in English.

Ajimu Farmstay NPO Ajimu Green Tourism Society (ajimu-ngt.jp) coordinates farmstay experiences for 60 families in Oita Prefecture, about 30 minutes from the hot-springs resort town of Beppu. Spend some time getting to know your hosts, try a little light farm work, and head out to explore the area. Ajimu is close to the lovely shrine of **Usa-jingu** and the ancient **Rokugo Manzan** temples hidden deep in the forested mountains.

Green Tea Homestay A double treat for those who love Japanese green tea: stay with a family of green-tea farmers in **Higashisonogi** (greentea-homestay.com) to learn and experience the green-tea production process. Tour the tea fields and factories and even learn how to pick and process tea yourself while getting to know the residents of rural Nagasaki.

Japanese Home Cooking

While harvesting your own ingredients for meals is one aspect of the farmstay experience, many farmstays also offer an opportunity to participate in the preparation of your meal, along with the host and any other guests staying at the same time.

For cooks and food lovers, this is a unique chance to experience how Japanese home-cooked meals are prepared, learn about other ingredients that are added to dishes and how to find them in local supermarkets – and with a bit of luck, receive a secret family recipe handed down for generations!

36 Island Getaway
TO GOTO

ISLANDS | OUTDOORS | HERITAGE

The picturesque Goto-retto (Goto Islands), off the coast of Nagasaki, have long flown under the radar as a travel destination. For those craving an island getaway with outdoor activities, creative accommodation options and a unique history, Goto is certainly worth a detour off the beaten path.

🗺️ How to

Getting here There are 40-minute flights from Nagasaki and Hakata airports to the main island, Fukue-jima. High-speed boats and ferries connect Nagasaki and Fukue ports; an overnight ferry leaves Hakata around midnight and arrives in Fukue just after 8am.

Getting around Rental cars are EV, with charging stations dotted around the islands' major attractions and city centre.

When to go Goto is a warmer-weather destination, so any time except winter. Summer is typhoon season, which can occasionally disrupt ferry and boat schedules.

Ways to Explore Goto

SUP Goto Leisure Provides stand-up paddleboarding adventures, or lessons for the newly initiated. Start in a glassy harbour with perfect conditions to learn the basics. After mastering the harbour, venture out and down the coastline to Kojushi Beach with an experienced guide.

Hiking The scenic hike to Osezaki Lighthouse is a favourite – short and steep, with commanding views of the rugged coastline of Fukue-jima. Several dormant volcanoes on the island offer easy hikes that reward you with panoramic views, including 315m-high Onidake, which can be hiked from sea level or a parking lot and observation point further up the mountain. Or explore the Abunze coastline, where dramatic lava rock formations rise from the calm blue sea.

Souvenir Ideas: Tsubaki Oil

Tsubaki (camellia) oil is an important product of Goto, both as a food additive and beauty product. It's considered a healthy oil, 100% natural and easily absorbed into the body. *Tsubaki*-oil cosmetics, soaps and cooking oil make good souvenirs to bring home.

Above left Beach, Goto-retto.
Above right *Tsubaki* oil.
Left Osezaki Lighthouse.

'Hidden Christian' heritage During the period of Japanese history when Christianity was banned by the shogunate, many Japanese Christians fled to Goto where they could live in relative safety, concealing their faith in the rituals of Buddhism. The ban was lifted in 1871, and many churches were built by the community of local believers who hid their faith for 250 years. **Dozaki Church** on Fukue-jima is a former church, now serving as a museum for Goto's 'hidden Christian' (*kakure Kirishitan* in Japanese) history. The island of Hisaka-jima is designated as a World Heritage Site for 'hidden Christianity' and can be reached by a short ferry ride. Naru-shima also has several sites, including the World Heritage Site of **Egami Church**. Many churches still function as places of worship, so reservations are required to visit.

🚲 Tour Goto by Bicycle

With its mild weather and long stretches of uncrowded scenic roads, Fukue-jima is a cyclist's dream.

Wondertrunk & co. (@wondertrunk_co) offers cycling tours of the island, led by tour coordinator and cycling guide William Liew.

Tours for beginners are under 25km and explore a variety of locations around the island. Customised tours for higher level cyclists are available; riders can plan them in advance by consulting with Wondertrunk & co. before arriving in Goto.

It's the only company in Goto renting cross bikes, so they can take you off-road to places other cycling tours don't cover.

Recommended by **William Liew**
Tour Coordinator and Cycling Guide
@wondertrunk_co

Map showing Goto-retto Islands with locations including Egami Church, Naru-shima, Narao, Hisaka-jima, Dozaki Church, Fukue-jima, Fukue, Shikoku Pilgrimage, SUP Goto Leisure, Arakawa, Onidake, Osezaki Lighthouse, Wondertrunk, Kojushi Beach, Tomie. Scale: 0–10 km / 0–5 miles.

Left Dozaki Church, Fukue-jima.
Below Egami Church, Naru-shima.

LEFT: YMZK-PHOTO /SHUTTERSTOCK ©;
RIGHT: JOHN S LANDER/LIGHTROCKET VIA GETTY IMAGES ©

A Temple Experience in Goto

Goto-retto was once an important stop along the route between China and Japan. Kukai (Kobo Daishi), the Japanese monk who brought Shingon Buddhism back to Japan from China, spent some time on the islands influencing local Buddhists before returning to Honshu. An 88-site pilgrimage, a scaled-down version of the famous Shikoku pilgrimage, can be done around Fukue-jima.

One of the temples on the pilgrimage is **Hoshoin**, the location of Oteragoto – an accommodation for up to three people adjacent to the temple building. The recently renovated section is modern and comfortable, with a fully stocked kitchen to use during your stay. The attentive owner can arrange an optional morning yoga session with a local instructor in the temple building, or guide you through simple sutra copying and meditation sessions. This is a casual temple experience you can enjoy at your own pace, not a deeply spiritual one that you might have in a place like Koya-san.

Listings

BEST OF THE REST

≋ Private Onsen

Hyotan Onsen

This Michelin-starred onsen in Kan'nawa, Beppu has 14 private coin-operated baths, and numerous unusual public baths, including a sand bath. On-site facilities include restaurants, so you can make a day of it.

Yuka

Nine private onsen hidden away in the forest of Kumamoto's Waita Onsen (p189). The seven standard-quality baths are large enough for a family of four and available 24/7. The two luxurious premium baths include both an indoor and outdoor bath and can be rented from 8am to 10pm.

Yamaga Onsen Seiryuso

A luxurious ryokan of northern Kumamoto perfect for couples. Some rooms have a beautiful private bath large enough for two and spacious hybrid Japanese-Western-style rooms.

Lamune Onsen

The novelty of this onsen in Oita Prefecture is its naturally carbonated water, though the facility's playful architecture adds to the fun. Three private baths are available on a first-come, first-served basis.

Sanso Tensui Ryokan

An upscale onsen experience in secluded environs of Oita, Sakuradaki (the waterfall that's a muse of Japanese artists) is steps away and can be seen from the *rotemburo* (outdoor bath). There are two open-air baths, two indoor baths and five reservable private baths.

≋ Unique Stays

Nishinokubo   ¥

The couple who run Nishinokubo, in Oita, are experienced with English-speaking foreign guests. Accommodation is in a separate building from the main house, with comfortable beds, sitting room and bathroom. Besides learning about the work they do on their farm, including harvesting shiitake mushrooms, learn how to make local specialities in the kitchen.

Ojika Kominka   ¥¥¥

The little Ojika-jima in Nagasaki Prefecture hosts six fully renovated *kominka* (Japanese folk houses) spread around the island that are simultaneously historical and luxurious. Cypress bathtubs, private Japanese gardens and views of the harbour are all possibilities depending on your choice of *kominka*.

⋒ Breathtaking Views

Daikanbo Aso Caldera Viewpoint

Best panoramic view of the enormous volcanic caldera and active Aso-san, in Kumamoto Prefecture. On a lucky day,

Takachiho Gorge.

KAN_KHAMPANYA/SHUTTERSTOCK ©

witness the 'Sea of Clouds' filling the caldera with the mountain rising from the centre. Hike from the parking lot to the overlook near the edge of the caldera for a different perspective.

Kokonoe Yume Suspension Bridge

This pedestrian suspension bridge in Oita offers a perfect view of two of Japan's most beautiful waterfalls – especially in autumn, when the foliage turns brilliant dappled shades of red, orange and yellow throughout the valley. At 173m above the valley floor, it's not for the squeamish.

Yunohira Observatory

The closest public viewpoint to Sakurajima, Japan's most active volcano. In the opposite direction, enjoy a sweeping view of Kagoshima on the other side of the bay.

◎ Must-See Historic Sites

Takachiho Gorge

A narrow gorge of otherworldly beauty in Miyazaki Prefecture. The *kagura,* a lively sacred dance telling the legendary story of Shinto sun goddess Amaterasu, is performed nightly in an abbreviated form at Takachiho-jinja, the ancient shrine near the gorge.

Yakushima

The island of Yakushima may be remote, but Yakushima National Park contains untouched forests of cedar that are over 7000 years old. This incredible natural habitat was the inspiration for the animated film *Princess Mononoke.* Arrive by boat or plane and spend the night on the island at one of the many hotels and inns along the coast.

Okubungo Course, Kyushu OLLE

This section of the Kyushu OLLE is a 12km walk that takes you through the heart of beautiful and historic Oita Prefecture. Starting from Asaji Station, pass through the ruins of Oka-jo, near towering Buddhist

Yunohira Observatory.

JESSE337/SHUTTERSTOCK ©

images carved into cliff faces, and through the samurai town of Taketa before arriving at Bungo-Taketa Station.

Arita, Okawachiyama & Imari

These adjacent towns of Saga Prefecture were responsible for the manufacture and export of Japan's first porcelain ceramics. Browse the shops and museums of these well-preserved towns, which include the Kyushu Ceramic Museum and Arita Porcelain Park.

✐ Made in Kyushu

Mamichan   ¥

One of the most popular of Fukuoka's *yatai,* the famous street-food stalls that come to life around the Naka-gawa every evening. It's a great introduction to *yatai,* with a variety of fantastic dishes.

Itoshima Oyster Huts   ¥

From roughly October to March, the port town of Itoshima has several dozen oyster-hut pop-up restaurants run by local fisher folk, which serve freshly harvested oysters and other seafood grilled by yourself at your own table.

Scan for more things to see, do and try in Kyushu

HOKKAIDO

OUTDOORS | NATURE | ADVENTURE

Experience
Hokkaido
online

HOKKAIDO
Trip Builder

▬▬▬ Japan's second-largest and most northerly island, Hokkaido almost feels like another country, a place where nature and adventure abound. Discover wide open spaces, untouched wilderness, a fascinating indigenous culture and some of the best powder snow in the world.

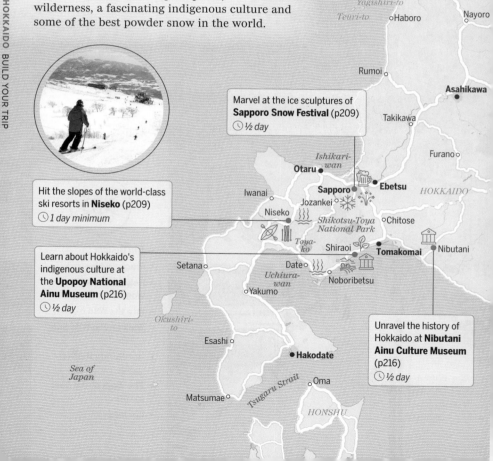

Marvel at the ice sculptures of **Sapporo Snow Festival** (p209)
🕐 ½ day

Hit the slopes of the world-class ski resorts in **Niseko** (p209)
🕐 1 day minimum

Learn about Hokkaido's indigenous culture at the **Upopoy National Ainu Museum** (p216)
🕐 ½ day

Unravel the history of Hokkaido at **Nibutani Ainu Culture Museum** (p216)
🕐 ½ day

Rebun-to
Wakkanai
Rishiri-to
Toyotomi
Yagishiri-to
Teuri-to
Haboro
Nayoro
Rumoi
Asahikawa
Takikawa
Furano
Ishikari-wan
Otaru
Sapporo
Ebetsu
HOKKAIDO
Iwanai
Jozankei
Niseko
Shikotsu-Toya National Park
Chitose
Toya-ko
Shiraoi
Tomakomai
Nibutani
Setana
Date
Uchiura-wan
Noboribetsu
Yakumo
Okushiri-to
Esashi
Hakodate
Oma
Sea of Japan
Matsumae
Tsugaru Strait
HONSHU

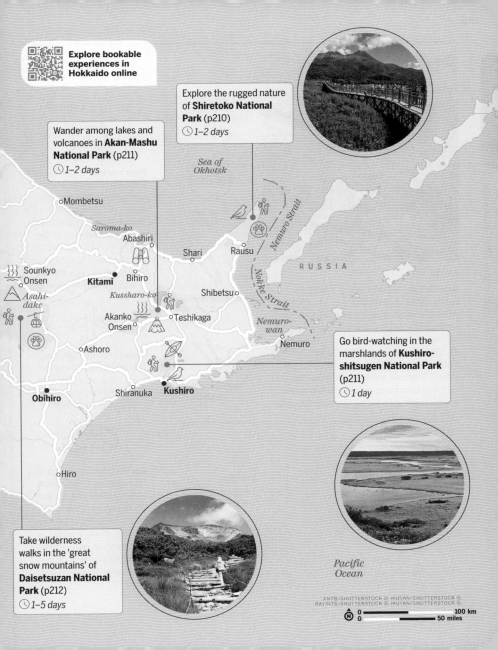

Explore bookable experiences in Hokkaido online

Explore the rugged nature of **Shiretoko National Park** (p210)
🕐 *1–2 days*

Wander among lakes and volcanoes in **Akan-Mashu National Park** (p211)
🕐 *1–2 days*

Mombetsu

Saroma-ko

Abashiri

Shari

Sea of Okhotsk

Rausu

Nemuro Strait

Notke Strait

R U S S I A

Sounkyo Onsen

Kitami

Bihiro

Kussharo-ko

Shibetsu

Asahi-dake

Akanko Onsen

Teshikaga

Nemuro-wan

Nemuro

Go bird-watching in the marshlands of **Kushiro-shitsugen National Park** (p211)
🕐 *1 day*

Ashoro

Obihiro

Shiranuka

Kushiro

Hiro

Take wilderness walks in the 'great snow mountains' of **Daisetsuzan National Park** (p212)
🕐 *1–5 days*

Pacific Ocean

ANT8/SHUTTERSTOCK ©, IKUYAN/SHUTTERSTOCK ©,
RAYINTS/SHUTTERSTOCK ©, IKUYAN/SHUTTERSTOCK ©.

0 — 100 km
0 — 50 miles

Practicalities

CHAYTANYAN/SHUTTERSTOCK ©

ARRIVING

New Chitose Airport The vast majority of visitors fly into New Chitose Airport, which is Hokkaido's main airport, located about 50km southeast of Sapporo. Trains run frequently between the airport and Sapporo (35 minutes, ¥1150) as well as buses (70 to 90 minutes, ¥1100) to various locations and hotels around the city. There are also train and direct bus links to other places in the region including Niseko, and car rental available directly from the airport.

HOW MUCH FOR

Soup curry
¥1200

Seafood rice bowl
¥1500

Jingisukan dinner
¥3000

GETTING AROUND

Train and bus Hokkaido has a more limited public transport network than many other regions of Japan, but there are good train and long-distance bus links between all the island's major cities. Local buses connect to rural spots, although service may be seasonal and infrequent.

Plane There are regular flights from Sapporo to regional airports around Hokkaido, but flights are sometimes cancelled in bad weather.

Car Renting a car is probably the best way to get around, especially if you plan on visiting fairly off-the-beaten-track places; take extreme care if driving in winter as conditions can be treacherous. Hokkaido is also a good destination for cycling tours.

WHEN TO GO

MAR–MAY
Snowy until April; spring blossoms not until the end of the month

JUN–AUG
Can be hot, but cooler and less humid than most of Japan

SEP–NOV
Getting cooler; first snow as early as mid-October

DEC–FEB
Very cold and often deep snow; February peak for winter activities

TOP: OKIMO/SHUTTERSTOCK ©
BOTTOM: VERONICA GALLERY/SHUTTERSTOCK ©

EATING & DRINKING

Local speciality Hokkaido is renowned for its fresh produce, dairy products and excellent seafood. The most famous regional dish is *jingisukan* – lamb or mutton (rarely eaten in other parts of Japan) barbecued with plenty of vegetables.

Seafood Hokkaido is said to have the best seafood in the country; be sure to try *kani* (crab), *ikura* (salmon roe) and the exquisite *uni* (sea urchin).

Winter warmers In the cold winter months a bowl of soup curry is a local favourite, along with ramen (especially rich and creamy butter ramen) – both go well with Sapporo beer.

Must-try ramen
Menya Saimi (p219)

Best seafood rice bowl
Takinami Shokudo (p219)

CONNECT & FIND YOUR WAY

Wi-fi Hokkaido has few free wi-fi spots compared to other areas of Japan (although it is available in many train stations and at New Chitose Airport), so it is best to rent pocket wi-fi (japan-wireless. com) to stay connected.

Tourist information The excellent Hokkaido Tourist Information Centre (tourist-information-center.jp/hokkaido) in central Sapporo can help you with any queries you might have.

TRAVEL PASS

There are a number of Hokkaido-specific travel passes; the Hokkaido Rail Pass allows unlimited trips on all JR trains (excluding the shinkansen; jrhokkaido.jp) and JR buses.

WHERE TO STAY

A wide choice of accommodation in the cities, and plentiful ryokan in rural hot-spring towns. In summer there are campsites, plus super basic (but cheap) rider houses for bikers and cyclists.

Place	Pro/Con
Sapporo	Hokkaido's biggest city. Central Sapporo is a transport hub; Susukino is the lively main nightlife district.
Niseko	Plenty of options, but book early during peak ski season. Summer is quiet.
Asahikawa	Second-largest city in Hokkaido; plentiful accommodation.
Hakodate	Gateway to Hokkaido by rail from the mainland and a good stop-off for awesome seafood, views and onsen.
Abashiri	Tiny city in eastern Hokkaido; good base for exploring Shiretoko and Akan-Mashu national parks.
Biel & Furano	Apartments near ski resorts; limited hotel and budget options.

MONEY

Be sure to carry cash at all times, especially if heading out into the wilds – while credit cards are widely accepted in larger cities, in rural areas cash is king.

37 Hokkaido's Winter
WONDERS

SNOW | SKIING | WINTER ACTIVITIES

■■■■ Hokkaido is a winter lover's dream – every season freezing Siberian weather fronts bury almost the entire island under a thick blanket of snow which remains for months on end. As a result, Hokkaido is home to some of Asia's top ski resorts and famous snow festivals and is the best place in Japan to experience a whole host of exciting winter activities.

WILLIAM CHU/GETTY IMAGES ©

🗺 How to

Getting around Trains, flights and buses operate throughout the winter, although expect delays after heavy snow storms. If driving, take extreme care and avoid the roads during snow storms and at night.

When to go Winter lasts from December until late

March, with February the best month for most activities.

Top tip Buy your ski pass in advance online (niseko.ne.jp). Also check snowjapan.com for up-to-date info on winter sports and snow conditions across Japan.

BONSTOCK/SHUTTERSTOCK ©

Above left Icebreaker, Abashiri.
Below left Dog sled, Furano.

Hokkaido Winter Tips

To comfortably enjoy the beauty of a Hokkaido winter, smart clothing choices for staying warm are a must.

Whether you're wandering around the Sapporo snow festival, snow-shoeing or skiing the side-country, layering is key. Think full thermal underwear, underlayer, mid-layer, thick outer layer with hood, high ankle warm boots, thick gloves and a woolly hat.

I also never head out without spare batteries for my smartphone, camera and other electronics. The cold will sap the juice fast.

Convenience stores everywhere have free boiling water on tap, so bring an insulated bottle to keep topped up with your own hot beverages.

By Rob Thomson
Lives in Sapporo and founder of HokkaidoWilds.org.
@hokkaidowilds

Super skiing Hokkaido's top winter sports destination, **Niseko** is renowned for its incredible powder snow, world-class slopes and remote back-country possibilities. With good access from Sapporo and the airport, the four main resorts of Hanazono, Grand Hirafu, Niseko Village and Annupuri fall under the moniker of Niseko United and encompass 30 lifts and around 60 runs in total, with an all-mountain pass and free shuttle buses providing unlimited access. English-speaking guides and foreign-run businesses give the area a vibrant, international feel.

Snow festivals Held for one week in early February, the **Sapporo Snow Festival** (Sapporo Yuki Matsuri) is a spectacular celebration featuring giant snow and ice sculptures, concerts and other events. Most of the action takes place at centrally located Odori Park where sculptures are lit up until 10pm, with more attractions dotted around town. Check out the winter festivals at Asahikawa and other places in Hokkaido around the same time too.

Winter fun If skiing and snowboarding don't float your boat then head to **Furano** and join a guided snow-shoeing tour. Alternatively, ride a snow mobile through the woods or try your hand at dog sledding (furanotourism.com).

Walking on ice In February, drift ice from Siberia floats down to the shores of **Mombetsu** and **Abashiri** in eastern Hokkaido, creating an amazing frozen seascape. Don a drysuit and go for an ice floe walk (en.visit-eastern-hokkaido.jp), or take an icebreaker cruise (ms-aurora.com) to witness this unique phenomenon.

38 Into the WILD

WILDLIFE | LANDSCAPE | BIRDWATCHING

Eastern Hokkaido is a land of vast open plains, pristine wetlands and rugged mountain refuges, where people are few and nature rules supreme. This tour takes in three spectacular and distinctly unique national parks, with the chance to see some of Hokkaido's most iconic and rare wildlife, including brown bears and Japanese cranes.

🗺️ How to

Getting here Fly from Sapporo and some other Japanese cities to Memanbetsu or Kushiro airports; rail and bus links with Sapporo and Asahikawa.

When to go All year, although wildlife and activities vary greatly depending on the season, and some things close in winter.

Getting around The JR Senmo (or 'Semmo') line links Abashiri, Kushiro and the national parks with connecting buses to popular spots during most seasons. Renting a car provides much more flexibility.

Natural wonder A true wilderness and World Heritage Site, **Shiretoko National Park** is a 70km-long peninsula packed with waterfalls, ancient forests and a mountainous interior for hardy hikers to explore – but beware, Shiretoko has the highest density of *higuma* (brown bears) in Hokkaido. Boat cruises along the coast offer the chance of spotting them from a safe distance, along with other wildlife such as whales and sea eagles. The beautiful Shiretoko Goko (five lakes) area has gentle nature walks.

Above right Japanese cranes.
Below right Brown bears, Shiretoko.

ONDREJ PROSICKY/SHUTTERSTOCK ©

🕊 Unmissable Wildlife

Shiretoko See bears, seals, whales, sea eagles, orcas and dolphins.

Akan-Mashu Look out for Yezo red foxes, brown bears and deer.

Kushiro-shitsugen Spot the Japanese crane, saved from near extinction in the early 20th century.

Fire and water The stunning **Akan-Mashu National Park** is an area of steaming volcanic peaks and serene lakes, one of which, Mashu-ko, is said to have the clearest water of any lake in the world! The lakeside hot-spring resort of Akanko Onsen lies between the volcanic summits of O-Akan-dake and Me-Akan-dake and Mount Meakan (both offer splendid hiking), while the small town of Kawayu Onsen is famed for its invigoratingly acidic hot springs.

Birding paradise Home to the Japanese crane and other rare flora and fauna, **Kushiro-shitsugen National Park** is Japan's largest wetland. There are observatories and trails throughout the park, and year-round kayak tours offer unique views of the marshlands and wildlife.

AZUKI25/GETTY IMAGES ©

39 Walk on the
WILD SIDE

HIKING | MOUNTAINS | NATIONAL PARK

Daisetsuzan is Japan's largest national park – a vast and untouched wilderness of spectacular mountains, alpine flower meadows, steaming volcanic landscapes and year-round snow fields. Hiking trails offer day and multi-day options, with the chance of encountering wildlife such as red foxes and brown bears. Abundant hot-spring baths provide a spot of relaxation pre- or post-hike.

T KINGFISHER/SHUTTERSTOCK ©

🗺 **How to**

Getting here Buses run from Asahikawa to Asahidake Onsen, and between other trailheads and various stations.

When to go Summer and autumn (beginning of July to early October) are best as trails will be mostly snow-free.

Maps The best English-language hiking map is *Asahi-dake: The Heart of the Daisetsuzan National Park*, which you can buy online. Alternatively, check hokkaidowilds.org for free downloadable and printable route maps.

CHEN MIN CHUN/SHUTTERSTOCK ©

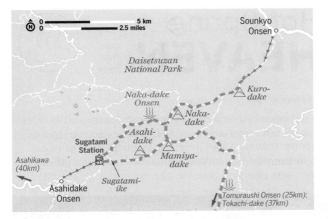

Above left Asahi-dake.
Below left Kuro-dake ropeway.

Volcanic views From Asahidake Onsen ride the ropeway up to Sugatami Station; from there it is a 20-minute walk to the mirror-like reflections of Sugatami Pond, where steam and volcanic gases spurt up from the earth. Then prepare for a gradual two-hour clamber up the scree slopes of Asahi-dake for far-reaching views (if the weather is kind) – at 2291m it is Hokkaido's highest mountain. Most hikers head back down to the ropeway the same way.

Into the wild A more demanding loop-hike option continues east from the summit of Asahi-dake, dropping down on loose rocks and snow, before turning left at Mamiya-dake. The trail then scoots down to the small natural hot spring at Naka-dake Onsen where you can take a rejuvenating mid-hike dip, before slinking back across boardwalks and grassy slopes to return to the ropeway (allow seven hours).

Multi-day trekking Well-equipped hikers can use huts and campsites for longer adventures – a good one- or two-day trek continues north–east from Asahi-dake, climbs Kuro-dake and finishes at Sounkyo Onsen. A challenging three-day option involves turning south after Asahi-dake and trekking through the heart of the national park, ending at the remote Tomuraushi Onsen. Truly hardcore hikers can opt for the full five-day Daisetsuzan traverse, continuing even further south through extremely remote and wild country all the way to Tokachi-dake.

🐾 Bear Necessities

Even when Sapporo is basking in summer heatwaves, the high, windswept ridges and changeable weather of Daisetsuzan can be bracingly cold, so warm layers and waterproof clothing are essential, especially for longer treks.

Mountain huts are basic, meaning trekkers will need to bring their own sleeping gear and food. Water is usually sourced from streams or snow patches (always boil or filter before drinking).

Bear encounters, while rare, are a possibility so carry a bear bell or make noise (clap and sing!) while on the trail to avoid a surprise meeting.

40 Hot-Spring
HEAVEN

HOT SPRINGS | CULTURE | RELAXATION

▰▰▰▰▰ Natural hot springs or onsen can be found throughout Japan, and soaking in their mineral-infused waters not only reinvigorates the body and soul but is a fundamental part of Japanese culture. From developed resort towns to rustic bathhouses and secret out-in-the-wild hot springs, Hokkaido is heaven for onsen lovers – here are some of the best places to take the plunge.

KORKUSUNG/SHUTTERSTOCK ©

🕮 **How to**

When to go Any time. Unwinding in a *rotemburo* (outdoor hot spring) surrounded by snow in winter is one of life's great pleasures.

Cost Usually ¥500 to ¥2000; highest at plush hotels and resorts.

Basic outdoor baths are often free or request a small fee to be left in an honesty box.

Take note Some onsen may not allow entry to people with tattoos, or require small tattoos to be covered up.

KRYSZTOF BARANOWSKI/GETTY IMAGES ©

Above left Oyunuma-gawa.
Below left Sounkyo Onsen.

Heaven and hell The most famous hot-spring resort in Hokkaido is **Noboribetsu Onsen**, mainly due to the various kinds of mineral-rich waters which are said to have healing properties. Most hot springs in the town are connected to hotels and ryokan which non-staying guests can enter, usually with a choice of indoor and outdoor baths.

Between soaks be sure to explore **Jigoku-dani**, a sulphur-stained 'hell valley' nestling just above town. From there, trails lead in 20 minutes to a thermally heated pond called Oyunuma – its outlet, the Oyunuma-gawa, is a steaming and otherworldly hot river flowing through the woods in which you can dip your feet, so bring a towel.

Mountain retreat Nestling in the mountains only an hour from Sapporo, **Jozankei Onsen** is a small hot-spring resort at the northern end of Shikotsu-Toya National Park. There are a number of large hotels each with their own hot springs, and the friendly staff at the town's information centre can offer recommendations. Just out of town, the large open-air bath at Hoheikyo (hoheikyo.co.jp) is often claimed to be one of Hokkaido's best.

Forest bathing Set in a scenic narrow valley among woodland, cliffs and waterfalls, **Sounkyo Onsen** is home to fancy hot-spring hotels and the Kuro-dake Ropeway, which is the northern gateway to Daisetsuzan National Park. It also hosts a popular two-month-long winter festival.

♨ Getting Into Hot Water

Entering an onsen for the first time can be a little intimidating, especially if you're not comfortable being naked in front of strangers, but the etiquette is quite straightforward.

Baths are usually gender segregated – look for the 女 (onna/female) and 男 (otoko/male) symbols. In the changing room, take off all your clothes (swimwear is generally not permitted) and put them in a basket along with your towel. You may, however, take in a small towel to protect your modesty.

Then, clean your body using the showers or washbowls, and rinse away all soap before entering the bath.

41

The Ways of
THE AINU

AINU | INDIGENOUS PEOPLE | NATIVE CULTURE

Only fully colonised by the Japanese as recently as the 19th century, Hokkaido has long been the home of the Ainu, the native people of the island. Once persecuted and marginalised to the fringes of society, moves are now being made to preserve the Ainu traditions and language. Here are a few places to learn more about their fascinating culture.

🗺 How to

Getting around Most places can be reached by public transport.

When to go Most facilities open all year, apart from a few days around New Year. Many museums are closed on Mondays (or the following day if Monday is a national holiday).

Fun fact A large number of place names in Hokkaido, including Sapporo, originate from the Ainu language.

National museum The **Upopoy National Ainu Museum** in Shiraoi is a lavish facility on the shores of Poroto-ko featuring exhibits related to all aspects of Ainu culture. The adjoining parkland has a reconstruction of an Ainu *kotan* (village).

In Sapporo check out the Hokkaido Museum and Sapporo Pirka Kotan (Ainu Culture Promotion Centre).

Ainu heartlands The Hidaka region is closely associated with the Ainu, and the fantastic **Nibutani Ainu Culture Museum** features a great collection of

Above right Traditional clothing displayed at the Hokkaido Museum of Northern Peoples, Abashiri.
Below right Upopoy National Ainu Museum, Shiraoi.

VARIOUS IMAGES/SHUTTERSTOCK ©

🏛 Ainu History

The Ainu are the indigenous inhabitants of Hokkaido and nearby regions. They lived as groups of hunter-gatherers and fisher folk, with their own language, customs and beliefs. After years of forced assimilation, the government has finally begun to recognise and protect Ainu culture.

exhibits and many traditional buildings – well worth visiting despite being slightly out of the way.

Further north in Asahikawa, the rustic **Kawamura Kane-to Ainu Memorial Museum** was built in 1916 by an Ainu chief and is the oldest Ainu museum in Japan – its photos from the early 20th century are particularly fascinating. Also check out Asahikawa City Museum which has many excellent displays.

To the east Eastern Hokkaido's best Ainu-related attraction is probably the **Hokkaido Museum of Northern Peoples** in Abashiri. Informative exhibits showcase various northern indigenous peoples, conveying the struggle of living in cold environments. Don't miss the free audio guide.

PIXHOUND/SHUTTERSTOCK ©

Listings

BEST OF THE REST

🎿 Skiing & Snowboarding

Moiwa

Located next door to Annupuri but not part of Niseko United, this small resort has three lifts and plenty of that famous Niseko powder, but is much quieter than its popular neighbours.

Rusutsu Ski Resort

Large ski resort spread over three mountains, with long, groomed trails and exciting powder runs. East of Niseko, not far from Toya-ko.

Sapporo Teine

Less than an hour from Sapporo, this popular ski resort was a venue in the 1972 Winter Olympics, and has a choice of beginner-friendly and more challenging slopes.

Furano Ski Resort

In central Hokkaido, Furano has a choice of easy, intermediate and expert runs through its magical birch forests, with plenty of direct buses from Sapporo during the ski season.

⛺ Scenic Camping Spots

Naka-Toya Campsite ¥

Scenic lakeside campground on the forested eastern shore of Toya-ko, with toilets on-site and hot springs close by.

Hoshi-ni-te-no-todoku Oka Campsite ¥

Open from April to October, this charming farm campsite overlooks the patchwork flower fields of Furano, with sheep sometimes wandering through camp. Tents, sleeping gear and bungalows for rent.

Nozuka Campground ¥

A free beachside campsite just a few minutes drive west of Nozuka on the rugged and beautiful Shakotan Peninsula. Basic facilities but wonderful seaside sunsets.

Kushukohan Camping Ground ¥

Situated on Rebun, a small island off the north coast of Hokkaido famous for its summer wild flowers. Large campsite with showers, next to a lake and the sea.

♨ Open-Air Hot Springs

Mizunashi Kaihin Onsen

Lying east of Hakodate on the rocky shore of Cape Esan, this unique hot spring in the sea only appears for a few hours at low tide. Mixed bathing, so bring a swimsuit.

Niseko Iroha

Hot-spring hotel at the foot of the Annupuri ski resort, with baths set amongst snowy Narnia-like woodland during winter. The water is said to have special beautifying qualities.

Kotan Onsen

A free-to-use outdoor bath with amazing lake views, right on the shores of Kussharo-ko in Akan-Mashu National Park. A large rock (barely) separates the genders, so swimwear is permitted.

YAMAO/SHUTTERSTOCK ©

Kotan Onsen.

Kamuiwakka Hot Falls

In the wilds of Shiretoko National Park, bathe beneath a waterfall heated by hot springs seeping into the river above. Take care scrambling up slippery rocks to reach it.

Beautiful Views

Hakodate-yama

This 334m-high mountain looms over Hakodate, a city built on a narrow isthmus in southwest Hokkaido. A ropeway to the summit leads to one of Japan's 'three best night views'.

Shirogane Blue Pond

A popular photo spot, this strikingly turquoise-coloured pond was formed accidentally after aluminium seeped into the water. It's a 20-minute drive from JR Biei Station.

Cape Kamui

Situated at the tip of the windy Shakotan Peninsula, a two-hour drive from Sapporo. Viewpoint with dramatic vistas of the cliffs and the famous 'Shakotan blue' waters below.

Mt Annupuri

Skiers know all about the jaw-dropping panorama of Yotei-zan, Niseko's Mt Fuji lookalike, and from the top of the Hirafu Summer Gondola there are equally fantastic green views.

Lake Mashu Observatory No 1

Viewpoint on the southwest side of Mashu-ko with outstanding views of the lake and the volcanic caldera of Mt Kamui. Especially breathtaking on a clear winter day.

Farm Tomita

The rolling flower meadows and lavender fields of Furano are a gorgeous sight in summer, and at this farm near Naka-Furano visitors can take photos while feasting on lavender ice cream.

Shirogane Blue Pond.

STRUCTURESXX/SHUTTERSTOCK ©

Regional Dishes & Specialities

Menya Saimi ¥

Sapporo ramen shop regarded as one of the best in the city, not far from Misono Station. Excellent miso ramen, but expect a wait.

Soup Curry Garaku ¥¥

Restaurant in Sapporo's Susukino district serving soup curry, a Hokkaido speciality. Various tasty bowls packed with fresh vegetables and your choice of spice levels, plus an English menu.

Takinami Shokudō ¥¥

Located in Otaru's Sankaku Market; try the *kaisendon* (seafood rice bowl), a cheap and satisfying way to sample an array of Hokkaido's fabulous fresh seafood in one sitting.

Jingisukan Daikokuya ¥¥

Popular restaurant in central Asahikawa specialising in one of Hokkaido's most famous dishes, *jingisukan* – succulent grilled lamb which you cook yourself along with an assortment of vegetables.

Scan for more things to see, do and try in Hokkaido

OKINAWA & THE SOUTHWEST ISLANDS

BEACHES | RYUKYUAN CULTURE | BEER

**Experience
Okinawa
online**

SHIKEMA/SHUTTERSTOCK ©

OKINAWA & THE SOUTHWEST ISLANDS
Trip Builder

Surf, swim and trek through the tropical paradise that is the southern islands. But don't forget to set aside time to learn about the culture, legends and legacy of this diverse corner of Japan.

Get a little dirty with a *dorozome* (mud dyeing) class on **Amami-Oshima** (p231)
🕐 ½ day

Admire the sweeping ocean views from the top of Amami-Oshima's **Miyakozaki** (p231)
🕐 ½ day

Explore Iriomote-jima's lush forests and mangroves on an **Urauchi-gawa cruise** (p229)
🕐 1 day

Spend a morning browsing the excellent food selection at Naha's **Makishi market** (p224)
🕐 ½ day

Go snorkelling on **Yonehara Beach** and watch Ishigaki-jima's colourful marine life (p228)
🕐 ½ day

Amami Islands
Koniya　Naze　*Kikai-jima*
Kakeroma-jima　*Amami-Oshima*
Tokunoshima　○Kametsu
Okinoerabu-jima　○Wadomari

Iheya-jima
Izena-jima
Ie-jima　Nago
Kume-jima　**Okinawa City**
Kerama Islands　**Naha**　*Okinawa-honto*

Ishigaki-jima　*Miyako Islands*
Hirara
Kubura　Ohara　**Ishigaki**　*Miyako-jima*
Yaeyama Islands

Explore bookable experiences in Okinawa online

TOKYO VISIONARY ROOM/SHUTTERSTOCK ©
PIXHOUND/SHUTTERSTOCK ©

0 — 200 km
0 — 100 miles

Practicalities

ARRIVING

Naha Airport 5km from central Naha, handles domestic and some international flights. The Yui Rail monorail offers direct access from the airport to many of Naha's attractions; a one-day pass costs ¥800.

CONNECT

Okinawa has Be.Okinawa Free Wi-Fi, a free wi-fi service available throughout the prefecture. It's easy to connect; just look out for the sign.

MONEY

Bring cash, as many of the region's smaller shops and restaurants don't take cards. Services like PayPay are generally accepted.

WHERE TO STAY

Place	Pro/Con
Naha	Central, downtown, with plenty of bars, nightlife and attractions.
Taketomi	Ishigaki-jima's traditional village; stunning nature and fascinating history.
Nago	The main retreat on Okinawa-honto, with excellent beaches and activities.

EATING & DRINKING

Okinawa soba Okinawa's take on the Japanese noodles staple is a ramen-udon-soba hybrid.

Orion beer The prefecture's most ubiquitous beer – light, crisp and refreshing.

Rafute Rich and juicy pork belly, loved by locals.

Must-try snack
Umi budo (sea grapes) (p225)

Best for browsing
Makishi public market (p224)

GETTING AROUND

Car The best way to get around all of the islands.

Scooter A fun option for those who want to travel like a local; avoid the rainy season.

Public transport Only recommended in Naha. For island escapes, opt for a bicycle.

DEC–FEB	**MAR–MAY**	**JUN–AUG**	**SEP–NOV**
Clear skies, mild temperatures, good for avoiding crowds	Great beach weather, sunny and clear, busiest season	Hot and humid, peak rainy season	Occasional rain, ideal beach temperatures

OKINAWA & THE SOUTHWEST ISLANDS FIND YOUR FEET

TOP: KENGO/SHUTTERSTOCK ©
BOTTOM: DAMADA/ SHUTTERSTOCK ©

42 Eat Your Way Around
THE ISLANDS

SEAFOOD | FUSION | AWAMORI

Okinawans are members of an exclusive 'blue zone' club, a recognised region of the world where the population lives much longer and healthier than average. So what does one of the world's longest-living and healthiest populations eat? It turns out it's purple potatoes, delicious bubbles plucked from the sea, plenty of sugar, and a special, local version of sake.

OKINAWA & THE SOUTHWEST ISLANDS EXPERIENCES

KENDONICE/GETTY IMAGES ©

How to

Getting around For easy food access, Okinawa-honto is the best. The island has a bus network but for more independence, rent a car.

When to go Typhoon season is May to early June, and the national holiday, Golden Week, is in April, so it's best to visit outside those dates.

Market-fresh Daichi Makishi Kosetsu Ichiba (kosetsu-ichiba.com), or Makishi public market, is a must-visit for excellent fish, vegetables and ambience.

SHARON COBO/SHUTTERSTOCK ©

MOMOMIMEE/SHUTTERSTOCK ©

Far left *Jimamidofu.*
Below left *Sata andagi.*
Near left *Beni imo.*

Izakaya staples Okinawa-speciality *izakaya* (pub-eateries) are easy to spot throughout Japan, with their unmistakable red, blue and white Orion-branded lanterns, and the same goes on their home island. Start the meal with a frosty glass of Orion, the local beer. Lighter than most lagers, on a warm summer evening it's perfectly paired with *umi budo* (sea grapes), a Western Pacific seaweed that looks like green caviar. These salty little bubbles, served with a vinegar-based sauce for dipping, are filled with ocean umami flavour. Be sure to try the sashimi – it's always fresh, delicious and cheaper than average.

For the love of pork On the southern islands, they love pork so much some people say, 'Okinawans use every part of the pig except its squeal.' It's a key ingredient of *rafute*, a braised pork slowly simmered in a sweet and savoury sauce, and *goya champuru*, a brightly flavoured stir-fry of pork, egg, tofu and goya (bitter melon).

Fresh take on a classic *Jimamidofu* and *okinawa-soba* are two examples of the island's reinventions of mainland Japanese staples. The former is tofu made from thickened, freshly squeezed peanut milk; the latter a regional take on Japanese soul food, with thicker, chewier noodles and topped with thick slices of pork. Taco rice, a dish of ground beef, salsa, lettuce and cheese on a bed of rice, came to popularity through US influence on the island in the 1950s.

🍬 A Little Sweetness

A region perfect for sugar production – rich brown sugar, to be precise – Okinawa is not the type of place to discourage a little sweet indulgence.

Sata andagi are like a reverse doughnut, deep-fried sugar-dusted balls of dough; they are a popular market snack, often also found at many tourist destinations.

For something a little more colourful, the island's *beni imo* (sweet potato) is a bright-purple dessert staple, and the *beni imo* tart is an icon of Japan's *omiyage* (souvenir) culture.

VTT STUDIO/SHUTTERSTOCK ©

Orion – Okinawa's Star Beer

A BREW THAT EMBODIES THE ISLANDS' SPIRIT

If Okinawa had official colours, they would be red, blue and white – like the ubiquitous lantern branding of the region's favourite brew, Orion. For many residents, this beer is more than just a way to cool down; it represents the spirit of the Southwest Islands.

What's in a Name

From its name to its flavour, ingredients and the story of its origin, Orion is an example of Japan's uncanny ability to imbue everything with a sense of purpose, philosophy and deeper meaning. The beer is named after the great Greek hunter who is immortalised as a constellation of stars visible from the southern hemisphere, but the name, which was selected by a public vote, is more than just a homage. According to the company, another reason the name was selected is the three-star emblem worn by the US forces governing Okinawa back when Orion was established.

Indeed, it's impossible to separate the brew from its origins: born in 1957 in Nago, on Okinawa-honto, during the American occupation of the islands, Orion was the creation of now-legendary Japanese businessman, Sosei Gushiken. Inspired to contribute to the reconstruction efforts of Okinawa, he founded the company to re-establish the island prefecture's identity while bottling – quite literally – the natural gifts of this subtropical region.

Okinawan Lager

Made with spring water sourced from Okinawa, Orion is a brew that was launched to match the climate and lifestyle of the Southwest Islands. Light and crisp, the palate of this rice-based lager was designed to accompany the mishmash cuisine of Okinawa, pairing equally well with bitter *goya champuru* as it does with American-inspired taco rice.

Left Orion-branded lanterns.
Centre Can of Orion beer.
Right *Goya champuru*.

Other parts of Japan have their eponymous brews, like Sapporo, but Orion – and its popularity – is different, a clear culinary and cultural separation from mainland Japan. Orion is an example of the prefecture's regional identity. The brand controls around 1% of the Japanese beer market but more than 50% of Okinawa's. Souvenir shops are stocked with T-shirts, towels and trinkets adorned with the Orion logo, the message being 'if you love Orion, you love Okinawa'.

> Made with spring water sourced from Okinawa, Orion is a brew that was launched to match the climate and lifestyle of the Southwest Islands.

The beer's influence on the island's culture goes far beyond the glass. Over its almost 65 years, the company has expanded into other industries. It is now responsible for local beachside resorts, like the Hotel Orion Motobu Resort and Spa; a golf club; a city hotel, Hotel Royal Orion; a manufacturing company, Orion Support; an annual beer festival, Orion Beer Fest; and a brewery-amusement-park hybrid, Orion Happy Park. From its humble beginnings as a local brewery to a ubiquitous name across the prefecture, Orion for many doesn't just represent a delicious light beer but a symbol of local pride, ingenuity and aspiration.

🍺 Beyond Beer

There's no question as to how much Okinawans love their beer – but for those not fond of the hoppy brew, there are alternatives. Orion produces a *chu-hai* (*shochu* highball) utilising local flavours like *shikuwasa* (Okinawan lime).

Awamori is another brew indigenous to the region; it's like a *shochu* (rice spirit), and it's produced from a unique local black *koji* mould and long-grain indica rice. Most folks enjoy it with a little water or on the rocks, but be prepared: it's powerful (30% to 60% proof).

43 Yaeyama Islands
ADVENTURE

TREK | DIVE | STARGAZE

Venture off the main island, Okinawa-honto, and you'll find an archipelago reaching from southern Kagoshima to Taiwan's doorstep. Iriomote-jima and Ishigaki-jima, part of the Yaeyama Islands family, are two of the biggest in this string of pristine tropical islands and both have unique appeal. Which island to explore is up to you, but we'd suggest visiting both.

🗺 How to

Getting here/around Japan's major airlines have regular flights between Naha Airport and Ishigaki Airport, the area's transport hub. Ishigaki Dream Tours and Yaeyama Kanko Ferry offer two routes. On the islands, car hire is the best option.

When to go Between November and May is the best time, as it's outside typhoon season.

Split appeal To make the most of both islands, focus on their strengths: Ishigaki-jima for white-sand beaches, Iriomote-jima for scenic wetlands.

Perfect view A white-sand beach with water so clear you can see shadows of the docked boats in the coral-replete seabed, **Kabira Bay** on Ishigaki-jima is home to popular glass-bottom boat tours, diving, and manta-ray spotting from April to October. Neighbouring **Yonehara Beach** is equally gorgeous and a little less busy, making it great for snorkelling. **Sukuji Beach**, to the northwest of Yonehara, is a haven for stand-up paddleboarding and families looking for fun in shallower waters.

Starry skies The centre of **Ishigaki-jima** is north of downtown, far enough from light pollution to make it

Above right Milky Way seen from Ishigaki-jima.
Below right Urauchi-gawa.

JANELLE ORTH/ALAMY STOCK PHOTO ©

OKINAWA & THE SOUTHWEST ISLANDS EXPERIENCES

🐾 Wildcat Spotting

The *yamaneko* is Iriomote-jima's spirit animal. Native to the island, this nocturnal wildcat was discovered in 1965. The island's development poses a threat to this elusive species – only a few hundred are left in existence. Homages to the *yamaneko* are found island-wide across everything from T-shirts to cars.

Local insight by Penny Wu
Travel Department's Supervisor of Customer Service at Yaeyama Kanko Ferry

an International Dark-Sky Association silver- and gold-tier recognised destination. Local organisations like the **Hirata Tourism** group (hirata-group.co.jp) run stargazing tours, but it's easy to spot the constellations without equipment on a clear night.

Forest trekking Iriomote-jima is dotted with mangrove swamps and deep-cut rivers. To see it up close, hop on a day-long return-trip jungle cruise down **Urauchi-gawa**, Okinawa's largest river. The boat will drop you off at a walking trail that leads into the lush forest. Along the river you'll find two almost horizontal waterfalls, **Mariyudo-no-taki** and **Kanpire-no-taki**, accessible via the trekking course.

PHOTOGRAPH BY PAUL ATKINSON/GETTY IMAGES ©

44 Amami-Oshima
ESCAPE

EAT | LEARN | SWIM

In any other country, Amami-Oshima – 'Amami' for short – would be a highly publicised, heavily trafficked tropical holiday destination. However, the combination of laid-back beach culture and Japanese humility has kept it under wraps. It's a place where giant turtles swim in the shallow waters; families pass down ancient mud-dyeing techniques; and local folk are working hard to keep the culture of Amami alive.

LUCY DAYMAN ©

PHOTONN/SHUTTERSTOCK ©

How to

Getting here/around
Regular direct flights from Tokyo, Osaka, Fukuoka, Kagoshima and Naha service Amami. On the island, it's best to rent a car or scooter.

When to go The weather is best from late June through August, but it can coincide with typhoon season (May and September) so flexible flights are key.

Beach stay Staying in Amami's northern Tatsugo region offers easy access to the most pristine beaches.

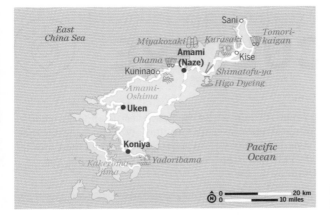

Above left *Dorozome* performed by Higo Dyeing.
Below left *Keihan*.

Beaches to begin The island's main feature are its stunning beaches, most of which sit along the northern third of the map. **Tomori-kaigan** is an excellent area for snorkelling and sea-turtle spotting. **Ohama**, near Naze, is another popular snorkelling beach with its coral reefs and vibrant aquatic life. The shallow waters and white sands of **Kurasaki** and **Yadoribama** beaches are sunbathing havens.

Taste the island Comfort foods that fuse mainland and south-island Japan are the culinary staples of Amami-Oshima. *Keihan* (chicken rice) is the island's best-known dish, available everywhere. It's a light combination of rice and colourful additions, including chicken strips, shiitake mushrooms and ginger, floating in a bowl of chicken broth. **Shimatofu-ya** is a popular tofu restaurant that will make any meat lover rethink their protein sources. This retro, Showa-period-styled store's cheap and massive lunch set draws groups of guests daily.

Material features Amami-Oshima is responsible for two traditional fashion forms. *Dorozome* is a process that sees the garment dyed in a yeddo hawthorn tree (*techi* in Amami dialect) dye before being soaked in the iron-rich field water. *Oshima tsumugi* uses those naturally dyed fabrics to weave splendid silk kimonos that boast a stunning depth of colour. There are a few collectives still practising *dorozome* on the island, such as **Higo Dyeing** (肥後染色). This workshop also runs classes for those not scared of a bit of manual labour.

🌊 Live Like a Local

A large portion of Amami-Oshima's population lives in small villages clustered throughout the island.

Kuninao, a village in the Yamato region, is a fascinating hamlet that blends laid-back beach culture with a rich sense of traditionalism.

NPO Tamasu (info@ amami.org) runs village and stand-up paddleboard tours guided by born and bred locals for those wanting an authentic view of the island – ask them to take you to **Miyakozaki** for some of the best views in Amami-Oshima.

45 Ryukyuan **CULTURE**

KARATE | CASTLES | SPIRITUALITY

▬▬▬ Of all the regions in Japan, Okinawa and the Southwest Islands have had one of the most unique coming-of-age stories. Before the 1600s, these picturesque islands were considered a separate country from Japan, one ruled by the Chinese-influenced Ryukyu kingdom. This rich in spirituality and responsible for the origins of karate, shaped Okinawa forever.

YANNICK LUTHY/ALAMY STOCK PHOTO ©

🗺 How to

Getting here/around
The most convenient way to get around Okinawa-honto is by car. To reach Kudaka-jima, take a ferry from Azama Port.

When to go Anytime outside typhoon season (May to early June).

What to say Think Japanese is hard? Ryukyuan languages have 10 distinct dialects. If you want to get in with the locals, try adding *mensore* (hello) and *nifei debiru* (thank you) to your vocab list.

THITINAN ANANCHAIPHATTANA/SHUTTERSTOCK ©

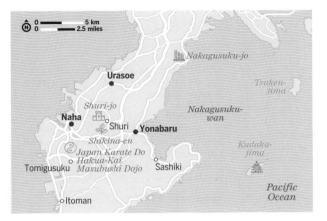

Above left Nakagusuku-jo.
Below left Shikina-en, Naha.

Royal history The symbol of Ryukyuan culture is Naha's **Shuri-jo**. Built in the late 1300s, the castle was the former capital, administrative centre and royal residence of the Ryukyu kingdom. Its uniquely Chinese-influenced design separates it from Japan's other castles. It was damaged during a 2019 fire, but its rebuilding will be completed by 2026.

Nakagusuku-jo is the most iconic of several castles built across Okinawa during the Ryukyu kingdom (pre-1879). While today only ruins remain, the castle's sections can still be quite clearly recognised, and the views of **Nakagusuku Bay** are spectacular.

Once a second residence to the Ryukyu kings, Naha's **Shikina-en** is a charming stroll garden that combines Ryukyu aesthetics with mainland Japanese design elements. A 300m circular path goes through the garden offering the perfect vantage point for admiring all angles of the park, from the forested area to the small islet in the middle of the park's pond.

Island of the gods With a circumference of just under 8km, **Kudaka-jima** is compact, but its size doesn't match its reputation. Kudaka-jima is known as 'the island of the god' because, according to Ryukyu legend, this is where the goddess Amamikyu first descended, making it the birthplace of the kingdom. It's only 15 minutes by high-speed ferry from Okinawa-honto and a perfect place to experience practically untouched Ryukyuan culture.

Way of the Hand

Okinawa is the home of karate – initially known colloquially as *te* (手), meaning 'hand' – and its roots are in the Ryukyuan culture.

For those looking to try their martial arts skills, there's a handful of schools running classes throughout the island. The long-running **Japan Karate Do Hakua-Kai Matsubushi Dojo** offers classes by Toshio-sensei and Agalawatta-sensei in two locations, with an option to take the classes in English or Japanese. While beginners of all ages are welcome, it's best to contact the school ahead of time to check whether pop-in is possible.

Listings

BEST OF THE REST

🌿 Spiritual Landmarks

Seifa Utaki

The island's most sacred destination, according to Okinawan legend, this corner of the Chinen Peninsula is where goddess Amamikyu came to populate the islands. Stroll the lush forest path and soak up the energy of this power spot.

Shuri Akagi

Near the cobblestone streets of Naha's Shuri Kinjo sits a cluster of six *akagi* trees, more than 200 years old. Lumpy and full of character, they survived the devastation of WWII and are said to be divine, as almost all of their siblings fell victim to the fires of war.

Daisekirinzan

Located in the northern part of Okinawa-honto, this jungle is known in Ryukyu mythology as an area overflowing with natural power.

Gangara Valley

These limestone caves in Nanjo are where people come to pray to find true love and admire a 20m-high banyan tree.

🖼️ Crafts & Culture

Ishigaki Pottery Studio

'Ishigaki Blue' is the term for this local variation of ceramics. By combining glass and pottery, artisans replicate the shades, depth of colour, and rhythm of Ishigaki-jima's surrounding waters.

Shiisa Park

Bright, bold and a little bombastic (in a good way), this public, mountain-backdropped garden near Yonehara Beach features a family of multicoloured, monster-sized *shiisa* (mythological Okinawan creatures). It's perfect for a photo opportunity and a short stroll on a sunny day.

Yaima-mura

An amusement park and open-air museum hybrid on Ishigaki-jima where local grannies teach traditional dance, relocated century-old homes built in Okinawan style stand proud, and fresh tropical fruit is in abundance.

Yaeyama Minsa

Learn all about Iriomote-jima's unique and fiercely protected *minsa* (weaving) style with a workshop visit. Historians estimate the fabric made its way to Okinawa from Afghanistan via China.

☀️ Relax & Recharge

Halekulani ¥¥¥

A combination of Okinawan flair and Hawaiian influence, this resort on Okinawa-honto is the epitome of the luxurious beach lifestyle. But there's more than just lounging around: guests can join a Halekulani Okinawa Escapes programme to learn about the island's culture.

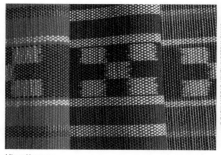

Minsa, Yaeyama.

CHRIS WILLSON/ALAMY STOCK PHOTO ©

Ryukyu Onsen Ryujin-no-yu

Embrace the onsen life surrounded by sand, not snow, with a soak in these natural hot springs near Naha Airport. With open-air baths allowing the soothing rhythm of the sea to wash over you, it's complete relaxation.

🍶 Awamori Icons

Sakaemachi Bottleneck ¥

You haven't tasted *awamori* (Okinawa's local liquor) until you've tasted it in a cosy, delightfully shabby *izakaya*, and Naha's Sakaemachi Bottleneck ticks all those boxes. *Awamori* options and food selections are equally abundant.

Bar Daisy ¥¥

It looks like a moodily lit, jazz-loving cocktail bar. But pay closer attention to the bottles in the bartender's hands and you'll notice they're switching out vodka and gin for *awamori* to craft artful cocktails. It's the perfect place in Naha to sample the south's signature spirit.

🥾 Hikes & Trails

Jawbone Ridge Loop

Looping around the mountains located near Kunigami on Okinawa-honto, this moderately challenging trail makes you work for its gifts – and it has plenty of them. Incredible view, excellent birdwatching and mysterious landmarks (keep an eye out for the abandoned hotel).

Hiji Otaki

An easy, almost 3km walk through the backtrails with waterfalls along the way near Kunigami, this hike offers two options; a river route or a forested trail. Entry comes with a fee, and the trail shuts at 4pm (3pm in winter), but it's a well-maintained and worthy mid-morning hike.

Daisekirinzan.

JORDAN TAN/SHUTTERSTOCK ©

OKINWAWA & THE SOUTHWEST ISLANDS REVIEWS

Indy Jones Mile

At just under 1.5km, this unforgettably named trail, located near Nanjo, is moderate in terms of challenge level and extreme in terms of beauty. With sweeping views, deep caves and the odd rope for climbing obstacles, Mr Jones would be proud to have his name attached to such a great adventure.

Scan for more things to do, see and try in Okinawa & the Southwest Islands

Practicalities

ARRIVING

238

GETTING AROUND

240

SAFE TRAVEL

242

MONEY

243

RESPONSIBLE TRAVEL

244

ACCOMMODATION

246

ESSENTIALS

248

LANGUAGE

250

Right Train journey near Mt Fuji.

EASY STEPS FROM THE AIRPORT TO THE CITY CENTRE

Most travellers to Japan arrive at Narita Airport, located about 60km from Tokyo's city centre. There are three terminals – international flights are divided between Terminals 1 and 2. The airport is well equipped with restaurants, shops, wi-fi rental kiosks, ATMs and luggage drop-off areas.

AT THE AIRPORT

NATTASAK BURANASIRI/SHUTTERSTOCK ©

Sim cards
Buy SIM cards at the airport, where you'll find a lot more variety than in the city. Vending machines are also available. Pocket wi-fi is a popular choice and flexible plans are available at Japan Wireless (japan-wireless. com).

Currency exchange
Available at bank counters at the airport upon arrival, or at automatic machines. Good rates for highly traded currencies like the US dollar. Visitors from countries in Southeast Asia will find more competitive rates back home.

Wi-fi Connect for free anywhere within the airport using FreeWiFi-NARITA. No sign-up or personal information required.

ATMs Withdraw money at the airport with your foreign bank card using SevenBank ATMs. Also available country-wide at 7-Eleven stores.

Charging stations Available at select locations (mostly departure halls and near terminals) and free to use. Japan uses a type A plug.

Customs declaration forms All travellers must fill this out. Forms are available at the baggage-claim area and are to be submitted to a customs officer before leaving. If you have unaccompanied mailed baggage, fill out two copies.
Duty-free Limits include three bottles (up to 2280mL) of alcohol, 200 cigarettes and 60mL perfume.

GETTING TO THE CITY CENTRE

Express trains The quickest way to get to the city (40 minutes). Choose between the Narita Express or Keisei Skyliner. Some walking or taxi to your final destination required.

Airport limousine buses Slower (1½ to two hours depending on traffic), but often service major hotels in the city so there's no transfer required. Guaranteed seat and luggage space.

Local trains The cheapest option, these are shared with regular commuters and can get crowded – best avoided when travelling with large baggage.

HOW MUCH FOR A

Express train
¥3000
40min

Bus
¥3500
1½–2hr

Local train
¥1200
1½–2hr

Commuter passes (Suica, Pasmo, ICOCA) The quickest way to board public transport and slightly cheaper than buying a ticket each time. Buy the pass at ticket-vending machines at any train station by putting down a ¥500 deposit that will be refunded upon return of the pass.

Price and validity period	How to use
Top up any amount starting from ¥500, whenever you please. The amount is good for 10 years from last use date.	Beep it at all station turnstiles. It can also be used to pay for goods at many stores, and when riding buses and taxis.

OTHER POINTS OF ENTRY

Haneda Airport is 30km from Tokyo's city centre, mostly for domestic flights and international flights to neighbouring countries. Take the express train to Shinagawa Station (¥410, 13 minutes) for easy transfer.

Kansai International Airport is 50km from Osaka's city centre. Take the train to Osaka Station (¥1060, 65 minutes) or to Kyoto (¥2850, 75 minutes). Buses are also available to either city.

Chubu Centrair International Airport is 50km from Nagoya's city centre. The Sky Limited Express goes to Meitetsu Nagoya Station (¥1230, 28 minutes). Ideal for exploring the Chubu region.

Fukuoka Airport gives easy access to all of Kyushu, Okinawa and the Southwest Islands. Take the subway to downtown Hakata (¥260, 10 minutes). Okinawa is a two-hour flight from here.

New Chitose Airport is Hokkaido's main airport, 50km from the city centre of Sapporo. Get to Sapporo Station by train (¥1150, 37 minutes) or bus (¥1100, 1½ hours depending on traffic).

TRANSPORT TIPS TO HELP YOU GET AROUND

You can explore a lot of Japan using public transport alone, but a rental car will unlock some otherwise inaccessible destinations while giving you more flexibility. Travel across prefectures quickly and (relatively) cheaply by shinkansen (bullet trains) or express trains, then hop on a bus or hire a car locally to explore at your own pace.

JR PASS A countrywide JR Pass starts from ¥29,650 for a seven-day period. This is ideal for taking the shinkansen across prefectures; hop on and off trains with no reservation required. Only valid for visitors on a tourist visa.

INSURANCE Car insurance is mandatory and can be applied for with the rental-car company when you make your booking or collect the vehicle. Plans come in a range of prices and can vary depending on the car; a basic plan is usually under ¥2000 per vehicle.

CAR HIRE
Major car-rental companies like Nissan and Toyota have offices in most towns; all offer similar rates. Smaller companies like Niconico (niconicorentacar.jp) can offer cheaper prices with older cars, but may not be as widely available in rural areas.

AUTOMOBILE ASSOCIATIONS
The Japan Automobile Federation (english.jaf.or.jp) has helpful resources for driving in Japan, such as information on traffic rules and emergency numbers. Breakdown assistance is available to FIA or AIT members. Have a valid membership card on hand.

CAR RENTAL PER DAY

per day ¥10,000

Petrol approx ¥150/litre

Insurance a day ¥1800

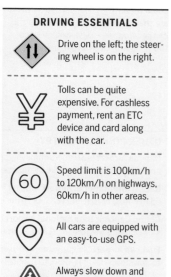

DRIVING ESSENTIALS

Drive on the left; the steering wheel is on the right.

Tolls can be quite expensive. For cashless payment, rent an ETC device and card along with the car.

Speed limit is 100km/h to 120km/h on highways, 60km/h in other areas.

All cars are equipped with an easy-to-use GPS.

Always slow down and stop for pedestrians at crossings.

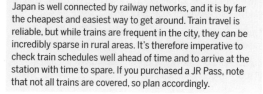

Japan is well connected by railway networks, and it is by far the cheapest and easiest way to get around. Train travel is reliable, but while trains are frequent in the city, they can be incredibly sparse in rural areas. It's therefore imperative to check train schedules well ahead of time and to arrive at the station with time to spare. If you purchased a JR Pass, note that not all trains are covered, so plan accordingly.

TRAINS Japan's trains are notoriously punctual, but there are some exceptions. Trains can be delayed by rough weather conditions such as strong winds and heavy snow, which can lead to extreme crowding at stations in Tokyo. Unforeseen circumstances like accidents can sometimes stop train lines entirely. While issues are usually resolved quickly, consider other options like taking a bus or taxi when these situations arise.

AIR Flying domestically can often be cheaper than taking the shinkansen. Most people fly to Hokkaido, Kyushu and Okinawa. You'll need more time travelling to and from airports, but it's a good option to save a bit of money.

COMMUTER PASSES Different regions have their own versions of commuter passes – Kansai primarily uses ICOCA, while Tokyo has Suica and Pasmo. If you already have one, there's no need to buy a separate regional one – they're all valid across Japan.

KNOW YOUR CARBON FOOTPRINT

A domestic flight from Tokyo to Fukuoka would emit about 350kg of carbon dioxide per passenger. A train would emit about 66kg, while a bus would emit 120 tonnes for the same distance.

There are a number of carbon calculators online. We use **Resurgence** (resurgence. org/resources/carbon-calculator.html).

VASIN LEE/SHUTTERSTOCK©

JAPAN GETTING AROUND

DANGER, ANNOYANCES & SAFETY

Low crime rates make Japan one of the safest countries in the world, but it's no excuse to let your guard down. Natural disasters are frequent, and it helps to stay vigilant and aware of emergency protocols.

TYPHOONS Typhoon season is July to October. Okinawa and the southern islands are more prone to them, while the main islands experience about three to four each year. A typical typhoon doesn't pose much risk, but severe cases can cause train lines in the city to delay or shut down, and lead to landslides and floods prompting evacuation. Check the Japan Meteorological Agency website (jma.go.jp) for warnings.

EARTHQUAKES & TSUNAMI Earthquakes are frequent, and visitors to coastal areas should be aware of tsunami warnings. If a high-magnitude earthquake or tsunami is expected, an advance warning will be automatically sent to mobile phones in the area. If a strong earthquake occurs, stay indoors and shelter under furniture unless instructed to evacuate.

VOLCANOES Many popular hiking destinations in the country are in fact active volcanoes – even Mt Fuji. Always be cautious when approaching one, and never venture into prohibited areas. Check the Japan Meteorological Agency for warnings before you go.

Bears are common in Japan's wilderness, particularly in Hokkaido. Stay alert when trekking at national parks, and watch out for bear warning signs. Carry bear repellent spray and travel in groups.

IMAGINGL/SHUTTERSTOCK ©

Smartphone App Get updated information on weather forecasts, disaster warnings and other helpful information on the app Safety Tips. It also includes a handy search for medical institutions in case of emergency.

STREET TOUTS
Do not follow a tout into any bars or *izakaya*, particularly in large entertainment districts like Shinjuku. These establishments tend to tack on shady charges to your final bill, and some may target tourists specifically.

INSURANCE
Clinics and hospitals don't take foreign health insurance, so you'll have to pay upfront. All pharmacies sell a wide variety of over-the-counter medicine for common ailments, though dosage is lower compared to what's found in other countries.

QUICK TIPS TO HELP YOU MANAGE YOUR MONEY

CREDIT CARDS Accepted in many shops in cities, but this isn't the case across the board. Many ramen shops, bars and small busitippnesses are cash-only. Visa payWave is available, but not commonly used. Visa and MasterCard are the most widely accepted, Diners Club and American Express cards less so. Many cashier counters in the city will have a sign showing the kinds of cards and payment options accepted.

CASH
Carry cash everywhere you go in Japan. Also have a coin pouch handy, because you'll inevitably end up with too many coins.

CASHLESS OPTION
Travellers can use their commuter-pass balance to pay for goods. All convenience stores and many chain restaurants accept them.

CURRENCY

Yen (¥)

HOW MUCH FOR A

Coffee ¥450

Onigiri (rice-ball snack) ¥120

Dinner for two ¥4000

TAX The consumption tax is 8% on takeaway food items and 10% for dining in and everything else. Tourists get a tax exemption on certain products with a value exceeding ¥5000 in a single receipt.

ATMS
Local Japanese bank ATMs don't accept foreign cards. Instead, look for SevenBank ATMs, found at almost every 7-Eleven are available 24hrs. ATMs are unavailable from 9pm to 12am on Sundays and public holidays.

CURRENCY EXCHANGE
The best way to exchange currency is at your home country or at the airport. Hotels, bank branches and department stores will exchange currency too, albeit at less favourable rates.

TIPPING Not required in Japan. Even if you insist, locals might refuse.

Restaurants Pay only the amount printed on your bill. Fancier restaurants will tack on a 10% service charge or a table charge. *Izakaya* (pub-eateries) may serve an obligatory appetiser and charge around ¥500.

Taxis Taxi drivers will always give your change back.

Guides Local guides don't expect tips, but may occasionally accept. When tipping, never hand money directly to them – instead, put the money in an envelope.

PAYING AT THE TILL
When paying, always set your credit card or cash on a tray placed in front of you. The cashier will also usually put your change back on the tray. When dining at a restaurant, a cash register at the front of the restaurant means you pay there after your meal.

RESPONSIBLE TRAVEL

Tips to leave a lighter footprint, support local and have a positive impact on local communities.

ON THE ROAD

Calculate your carbon footprint
Try an online carbon calculator
(resurgence.org/resources/
carbon-calculator.html).

Choose an EV EVs are slightly
cheaper to rent than a standard
vehicle. Online booking available
in English at nissan-rentacar.jp.

Rest stops are spaced along
the highway and will have bathrooms and bins to throw out your
rubbish.

Reusable bags and cutlery
Decline bags and cutlery by
saying *'Sono mama de daijoubu
desu'* (It's fine as it is).

Public bins These are scarce,
leave some room in your bag to
stash your rubbish until you find
somewhere to dispose of it.

Carry a water bottle Tap water
in Japan is safe to drink, but many
Muji stores (muji.com) around the
country have free filtered water
refill stations.

Public transport systems These
are well established across the
country, and discount passes
make them easier on your
wallet too.

OKIMO/SHUTTERSTOCK©

GIVE BACK

Try some taco rice and help kids in need Taco Rice Lovers
(tacorice-lovers.okinawa) partners with local restaurants to
feed children who go without a meal. When you eat taco rice at a
participating restaurant in Okinawa, purchase a Mirai Ticket along
with your meal. A child can then use the ticket to get a free taco
rice meal.

Help clean up Tokyo's rivers Join group volunteer efforts and make
some friends along the way. Tokyo River Friends (tokyoriverfriends.
org) hosts multiple clean-up events each month.

Support wildlife Make a donation to wildlife conservation and animal
welfare in Japan by donating to the Japan Wildlife Conservation
Society (jwcs.org) or Animal Refuge Kansai (arkbark.net).

DOS & DON'TS

Do take your shoes off when entering some temple halls.

Don't take anyone's photograph without asking permission and always respect locals' privacy. This not only applies to geisha, *maiko*, priests and shrine maidens, but also everywhere in public.

Do keep voices low when on public transport.

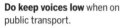

LEAVE A SMALL FOOTPRINT

Low impact transport See more of the city and discover lesser travelled areas on a bike. Docomo Cycle bikes (docomo-cycle.jp) are red and can be found in major cities across the country. Download the app to locate and rent bikes.

Go rural The most beautiful parts of Japan are often rural — experience ecofriendly farmstays, see the sights, then meet some locals and support small businesses too.

Try WWOOFing Make lasting connections while getting your hands dirty with the locals. You'll also be directly supporting local agriculture (wwoofjapan.com).

Eco-friendly cutlery Pick up a pair of bento chopsticks or cutlery (usually in cute designs and a small case) as a fun away to avoid using disposables.

SUPPORT LOCAL

Stop for tea or buy snacks from small businesses to support local economies.

Sustainable fashion When choosing a souvenir, consider buying old kimonos from second-hand shops. In Tokyo, they can be found in neighbourhoods like Nakano and Koenji.

Local crafts Make unique gifts to take home and also support local artists when you buy directly from their shops or sign up for a workshop.

PIXHOUND/SHUTTERSTOCK ©

JAPAN POSITIVE-IMPACT TRAVEL

CLIMATE CHANGE & TRAVEL

It's impossible to ignore the impact we have when travelling, and the importance of making changes where we can. Lonely Planet urges all travellers to engage with their travel carbon footprint. There are many carbon calculators online that allow travellers to estimate the carbon emissions generated by their journey; try resurgence.org/resources/carbon-calculator.html. Many airlines and booking sites offer travellers the option of offsetting the impact of greenhouse gas emissions by contributing to climate-friendly initiatives around the world. We continue to offset the carbon footprint of all Lonely Planet staff travel, while recognising this is a mitigation more than a solution.

RESOURCES
wwoofjapan.com
zenbird.media
japanfs.org
ecotourism.gr.jp

UNIQUE & LOCAL WAYS TO STAY

Hotels and ryokan aren't just places to stay – they're where Japan's spirit of hospitality, omotenashi, comes to life. A night at a ryokan and soak in an onsen after dinner is an experience every traveller must have at least once. Get to know the locals when you book a farmstay; for a taste of the unique and futuristic, try bunking at a capsule hotel.

JAPAN ACCOMMODATION

HOW MUCH FOR A

Capsule hotel
¥5000/night

Ryokan
¥12,000/night

Farmstay
¥9000/night

MR JAMES KELLEY/SHUTTERSTOCK ©

FARMSTAYS This is the way to go if you're looking for a place to rest as well as to experience the local way of life. There are farmstays sprinkled across the country – by the coast, at the foot of mountains, near hot springs and even at tea farms. You'll be staying with a local family in their home and dining with them too, so it's the opportunity to make lasting connections. Not all hosts are fluent in English, but if they're used to hosting tourists, they might be.

From ¥8000 to ¥10,000 per night/adult.

CAPSULE HOTELS
Hallways lined with pods designed to house a bed, a single person and very little else – the capsule hotel certainly isn't for the claustrophobic. The upside is that you'll get plenty of privacy, and they're often in central city locations. Amenities are provided, and facilities are good, clean and well maintained.

Around ¥3000 per night/adult.

LIGHT RECORDS/SHUTTERSTOCK ©

GLAMPING The 'glamorous camping' trend has become quite popular in Japan in recent years. Guests can book high-end tents with hotel-like facilities; campgrounds sometimes have a bathhouse too. While it's not cheap, stepping out of your cosy bed and being greeted by fresh mountain air and expansive views is well worth the price.

From ¥25,000 per night/adult.

GREG ELMS/LONELY PLANET ©

THE RYOKAN EXPERIENCE

Kaiseki dinner The fee will always include *kaiseki* (Japanese course-style dinner), served either in a dining hall with other guests or in the privacy of your own room. Every ryokan has its speciality, usually featuring a premium local ingredient.

Yukata Sets of *yukata* (light kimono-like robes) can be found in your room. These are for guests to wear when lounging around, and many wear them to dinner in the hall. Don't be afraid to ask for help putting it on; put the left side of the robe over the right – you should be able to insert your right hand between the folds.

Onsen The main bathing facility at a ryokan may be shared between all guests, so you may have to get naked with strangers – no swimsuits allowed. Always wash yourself before going in. If you have large tattoos or want more privacy, some ryokan offer rooms with private baths.

RYOKAN

On a trip anywhere in the country, a stay at a ryokan (traditional Japanese inn) is something many locals look forward to. They're easy to find, but are especially ubiquitous in hot-spring towns. These days, ryokan come in different forms: some are decades- or even centuries-old traditional establishments, but modern hotel-like buildings that retain the feel of lodging at a traditional inn are also considered ryokan.

From ¥10,000 per night/adult.

BOOKING

The best way to find and book accommodation is online and through travel organisations or websites. Be aware that some accommodation options, especially in rural areas, may not have foreign-language support.

Book in advance for the following seasons: Lunar New Year (late January to early February), cherry-blossom season (late March to early April), Golden Week holidays (late April to early May), Obon (mid-August), autumn foliage season (late October through November), and in winter (from December) for places like Shirakawa-go and Hokkaido.

Japan Ryokan and Hotel Association (ryokan.or.jp) Search hotels and ryokan across the country and compare prices between major booking companies.

Relux (rlx.jp) Find and book luxury hotels and ryokan.

Stay Japan (stayjapan.com) Book farm- and homestays across Japan.

JapaniCan (japanican.com) Easy booking for hotels, ryokan and guesthouses.

Japanese Guest Houses (japaneseguesthouses.com) Book farmstays and ryokan.

PRICING

Because your package will always include up to two meals, ryokan and farmstay prices are always listed as per person. At a ryokan, a small bathing tax will also be added to your bill (typically ¥150 per person).

248

 ESSENTIAL NUTS-&-BOLTS

TATTOOS
Public baths and spas often don't allow entry if you have large tattoos. If yours is small enough, some places give you a sticker to cover it up.

SMOKING
Many bars and clubs allow smoking. Some restaurants have smoking rooms. In public, only smoke at designated areas and not on the street.

TAXIS
There's no need to open or close taxi doors. Stand clear while the driver operates them.

FAST FACTS

Time Zone
GMT+9

Country Code
81

Electricity
100V,
50Hz/60Hz

GOOD TO KNOW

Citizens from 68 countries are automatically issued a tourist visa upon arrival, valid for 15 to 90 days.

Tourist-visa holders enjoy duty-free shopping at many retailers for purchase amounts exceeding ¥5000.

The legal drinking age in Japan is 20.

Never stand side by side on an escalator. Keep to one side; follow the lead of the person in front of you.

Public dustbins are rare. Carry your trash with you until you find one, and always sort trash and recyclables.

ACCESSIBLE TRAVEL

Accessible Japan (accessible-japan. com) is a great resource to help prepare for your trip.

Elevators are found at most city stations. Station staff will help you get on and off the train with a temporary slope.

Some train cars have wider areas meant for wheelchairs. Symbols for these cars are clearly marked on the platform.

Multipurpose toilets are common and can be found at stations, tourist destinations, shopping malls and public spaces.

Bmaps is an app that can help you find accessible dining options, locate bathrooms, and gauge the accessibility of an area before you go.

WATER

Tap water in Japan is completely safe to drink, though bottled water is inexpensive (¥100).

STATION EXITS

Look up the ones closest to your destination. Taking the wrong exit may lead to unwanted detours.

BATHHOUSE RULES

No clothes (including swimwear) allowed in some onsen. Children up to age seven can accompany either parent, regardless of gender.

FAMILY TRAVEL

Dining Family restaurants like Royal Host, Denny's and Saizeriya have kids menus and baby chairs.

Toilets and changing areas Most department stores and stations have multipurpose toilets, with a baby seat and diaper changing area.

Transport Children 12 and under pay half price for train rides. Up to two children under six years can ride trains for free.

Attractions Children under 12 get ticket discounts, and young children sometimes get in for free.

TOILETS

In the city are Western-style and have bidet features. Squat toilets are rare, and are indicated by a symbol placed outside the cubicle. In rural areas, squat toilets are more common. Some women's toilets have speakers that play a flushing sound; this is to mask other less favourable noises.

TIPS TO SAVE MONEY

- Snag discounted food at supermarkets in the evening.
- Visit karaoke boxes on a weekday afternoon.
- Ditch expensive onsen and go to a public bathhouse *(sento)* instead.
- Walk from one train station to the next; in Tokyo, this only takes 15 to 20 minutes.

MATIJA KROG/SHUTTERSTOCK©

LGBTIQ+ TRAVELLERS

Discrimination is rare, but society remains conservative when it comes to public displays of affection, regardless of sexual orientation.

Shinjuku Ni-chome in Tokyo is the largest LGBTIQ+ neighbourhood, with lively bars, clubs and entertainment. Engaging in public displays of affection here is generally fine.

Doyama-cho in Osaka is another nightlife area similar to Shinjuku Ni-chome.

Tokyo Rainbow Pride (tokyorainbowpride.com) is the country's largest LGBTIQ+ event and takes place in spring.

Stonewall Japan (stonewalljapan.org) is a good online resource.

文A LANGUAGE

Japanese pronunciation is easy for English speakers, as most of its sounds are also found in English. Note though that it's important to make the distinction between short and long vowels, as vowel length can change the meaning of a word. The long vowels (ā, ē, ī, ō, ū) should be held twice as long as the short ones. All syllables in a word are pronounced fairly evenly in Japanese. If you read our pronunciation guides as if they were English, you'll be understood.

To enhance your trip with a phrasebook, visit **shop.lonelyplanet.com**.

BASICS

Hello.	こんにちは。	kon·ni·chi·wa
Goodbye.	さようなら。	sa·yō·na·ra
Yes.	はい。	hai
No.	いいえ。	ī·e
Please.	ください。	ku·da·sai
Thank you.	ありがとう。	a·ri·ga·tō
Excuse me.	すみません。	su·mi·ma·sen
Sorry.	ごめんなさい。	go·men·na·sai

What's your name?
お名前は
何ですか？
o·na·ma·e wa
nan desu ka

My name is ...
私の
名前は...です。
wa·ta·shi no
na·ma·e wa ... desu

Do you speak English?
英語が
話せますか？
ē·go ga
ha·na·se·masu ka

I don't understand.
わかりません。
wa·ka·ri·ma·sen

TIME & NUMBERS

What time is it?	何時ですか？	nan·ji desu ka
It's (10) o'clock.	(10)時です。	(jū)·ji desu
Half past (10).	(10)時半です。	(jū)·ji han desu

morning	朝	a·sa
afternoon	午後	go·go
evening	夕方	yū·ga·ta
yesterday	きのう	ki·nō
today	今日	kyō
tomorrow	明日	a·shi·ta

1	一	i·chi	6	六	ro·ku
2	二	ni	7	七	shi·chi/na·na
3	三	san	8	八	ha·chi
4	四	shi/yon	9	九	ku/kyū
5	五	go	10	十	jū

EMERGENCIES

Help!	たすけて！	tasu·ke·te
Go away!	離れろ！	ha·na·re·ro
Call the police!	警察を呼んで！	kē·sa·tsu o yon·de
Call a doctor!	医者を呼んで！	i·sha o yon·de
I'm lost.	迷いました。	ma·yoi·mashi·ta

Index

WINNIE TAN

Winnie took a trip from her hometown of Kuala Lumpur to Tokyo one summer and decided she never wanted to leave. She has since spent seven years living in Tokyo, and hosts a podcast called *Monogatari: Tales from Japan*.

@weeniemon

My favourite experience is the snowy villages of Shirakawa-go. Seeing the villages and *gassho-zukuri* huts covered in snow is one of my fondest travel memories.

TED TAYLOR

Ted followed his interests in Zen and the martial arts to Japan in 1994. He has walked and guided many of Japan's old roads and pilgrimage paths, and has travelled widely across remote Asia. His work has appeared in numerous publications worldwide. See www.notesfromthenog.blogsport.com.

My favourite experience is walking the hills that ring Kyoto, dropping from its ancient forests into remote parts of the city.

THIS BOOK

Design development
Lauren Egan, Tina Garcia, Fergal Condon

Content development
Anne Mason

Cartography development
Wayne Murphy, Katerina Pavkova

Production development
Mario D'Arco, Dan Moore,

Sandie Kestell, Virginia Moreno, Juan Winata

Series development leadership
Liz Heynes, Darren O'Connell, Piers Pickard, Chris Zeiher

Commissioning editor
Sandie Kestell

Product editor
Claire Rourke

Assisting editors
Mani Ramaswamy, Brana Vladisavljevic

Cartographers
Corey Hutchison, Anthony Phelan

Book designer
Gwen Cotter

Cover researcher
Lauren Egan

Thanks
James Appleton, Fergal Condon, Clare Healy, Amy Lynch, Gabrielle Stefanos, John Taufa

Our Writers

LUCY DAYMAN

Australian-born Lucy was a music journalist before moving to Tokyo on a whim and never leaving. She believes that Japan's islands are just as good as – if not better than – its ski fields on the world stage.

@ @lucy.dayman

My favourite experience is casually swimming with wild sea turtles on a deserted beach on the northern coast of Amami-Oshima.

TOM FAY

Tom is a British travel and outdoors writer based in Japan since 2007. He is the lead author of a guidebook to hiking in the Japan Alps and Mt Fuji, and is working on a guidebook to Hokkaido. See www.thomasfay.com

@ @tomfay.jp
🐦 @T_in_Japan

My favourite experience is trekking through the wilderness of Daisetsuzan National Park – the remote and stunning scenery is some of the best in Japan.

TODD FONG

Born in California, Todd is based in the Tokyo area and travels up and down Japan on writing and photography assignments. His current obsession is sampling all different types of barrel-aged *shoyu* (soy sauce) brewed around the country.

@ @toddfong_travel

My favourite experience is waking up early after glamping on the Goto Islands' Nordisk Village and capturing the sunrise over the rice paddies with my drone.

REBECCA MILNER

Rebecca writes and edits from her sunny apartment in Tokyo, where she has lived since 2002. She has an MA in Japanese Studies from Sophia University in Tokyo and has contributed to more than 20 titles for Lonely Planet.

🐦 @tokyorebecca

My favourite experience is hiking the Kumano Kodo, in remote Wakayama Prefecture. It's already a great hike, but the culture and history make it fascinating as well.

Although the authors and Lonely Planet have taken all reasonable care in preparing this book, we make no warranty about the accuracy or completeness of its content and, to the maximum extent permitted, disclaim all liability arising from its use.

All rights reserved. No part of this publication may be copied, stored in a retrieval system, or transmitted in any form by any means, electronic, mechanical, recording or otherwise, except brief extracts for the purpose of review, and no part of this publication may be sold or hired, without the written permission of the publisher. Lonely Planet and the Lonely Planet logo are trademarks of Lonely Planet and are registered in the US Patent and Trademark Office and in other countries. Lonely Planet does not allow its name or logo to be appropriated by commercial establishments, such as retailers, restaurants or hotels. Please let us know of any misuses: lonelyplanet.com/ip.